THE DISTRIBUTION OF INCOME IN IRELAND

Brian Nolan, Bertrand Maître,
Donal O'Neill and Olive Sweetman

Oak Tree Press
Dublin
in association with
Combat Poverty Agency

Oak Tree Press
Merrion Building
Lower Merrion Street
Dublin 2, Ireland
www.oaktreepress.com

© 2000 Combat Poverty Agency

A catalogue record of this book is
available from the British Library.

ISBN 1 86076 208-5

This study forms part of the Combat Poverty Agency's Research Series,
in which it is No. 32. The views expressed in this report are the authors'
own and not necessarily those of the Combat Poverty Agency.

Printed in the Republic of Ireland
by Colour Books Ltd.

Contents

List of Tables and Figures

Acknowledgements

This study draws extensively on the 1994, 1997 and 1998 Waves of the *Living in Ireland Survey*, the Irish element of the European Community Household Panel. James Williams and Dorothy Watson were responsible for the survey design, data collection and database creation for 1997 and 1998, while the 1994 design, data collection and database creation were the responsibility of Brendan Whelan and James Williams. The authors are greatly in their debt. We are also grateful to colleagues in the ESRI and NUI Maynooth for valuable discussions on the issues and findings in a variety of forums, and to participants at the Irish Economic Association Annual conferences in 1998 and 2000 and the International Association for the Review of Income and Wealth, 25th Anniversary Conference, Cambridge, UK, 1998. Very helpful comments on earlier drafts were also received from Helen Johnston of the Combat Poverty Agency.

Foreword

INTRODUCTION

The Combat Poverty Agency is a statutory body working toward the elimination and prevention of poverty in Ireland. One of the Agency's key functions is to undertake research into the causes and consequences of poverty with a view to understanding how poverty can be overcome. The Agency also has a statutory role to provide policy advice to government and in this regard research findings are extremely important in helping us identify policy options and directions.

This research report examines the very important issue of income distribution. It examines how income is spread across households, looking at the gap between rich and poor and the factors which can operate either to narrow or widen that gap, and it identifies how Ireland fares on these issues relative to other EU and developed OECD countries.

The findings show that while Ireland has become increasingly wealthy in recent years, it still has one of the highest levels of income inequality in the EU. It is clear that our unprecedented economic growth is not lifting all boats in an equitable manner, and that better-off households are gaining from the boom to a greater extent that those who are less well off. These findings are of great concern to the Agency.

The growing gap between rich and poor during our economic turnaround is damaging to society in a number of ways. Firstly, given the broad acceptance that poverty in developed societies is a relative concept, it is still likely that there will be a link between the scale of income inequality and the levels of relative income poverty, i.e. greater inequality will result in greater poverty. Secondly, from a social justice or moral point of view, it is unfair or simply wrong that the benefits of economic growth are not shared more equitably, and that those who have most, benefit to a greater extent. Thirdly, income inequality is bad for social cohesion and inclusion, leading to alienation of marginalised groups, and the high social costs that this alienation or marginalisation can impose. Fourthly, severe income inequality limits choice and diversity, and hinders the ability of those on low incomes to participate fully in the political, social, economic and cultural life of society. This is a curtailment of basic rights and is contrary to the principles and objectives of the Government's National Anti-Poverty Strategy (NAPS). Fifthly, it also appears from research in epidemiology that income inequality is bad for a nation's health and that the healthiest nations are not necessarily the richest ones, but the ones where there is the smallest gap between rich and poor.[1] Finally, it is now being argued by economists that income inequality itself can be bad for economic growth.[2]

Severe income inequality implies a poor redistribution of resources and opportunities throughout society. If public policy does not intervene sufficiently to redistribute resources generated by the market, this in turn this implies a poor rate of public investment in social and human capital, and in public service and infrastructural development, all of which are essential to the long-term viability and sustainability of current economic good fortune.

Whether the motivation is the reduction of poverty, the pursuit of social justice, a concern for greater social inclusion or a commitment to economic growth, reducing income disparities is a necessary public policy objective.

The Combat Poverty Agency believes that a radical income redistribution in favour of those on low incomes is central to reducing poverty and creating an inclusive society — and later in

---

[1] Wilkinson, R. (1996) *Unhealthy Societies: The Affliction of Inequality*. London: Routledge.

[2] Persson, T. and G. Tabellini (2000) "Is Inequality Harmful for Growth?", *The American Economic Review*, Vol. 84, No. 3.

this foreword particular policy proposals are identified drawing on the lessons from the report's findings. The Agency's current strategic plan (1999-2001) identifies narrowing the gap between rich and poor as one of its four key strategic objectives, and suggests in a series of strategic goals, how this may be achieved through a fairer distribution of resources, services and employment opportunities in favour of people living in poverty.[3]

POLICY CONTEXT

This interest in a fairer distribution of income is not unique to the Agency, but is a view reflected throughout the current public policy arena, both at national and international levels.
The National Anti-Poverty Strategy (NAPS), the official government policy on tackling poverty, commits the Government to

> . . . ensuring that the impact of very rapid economic, social and demographic change reduces social inequalities and social polarisation . . . (and) that the benefits of sound economic management and growth are distributed fairly and in particular are used to tackle the underlying causes of poverty and social exclusion (Government of Ireland, 1997: 2).[4]

The *Action Programme for the Millennium*, the current government action programme, aspires to everyone sharing the benefits of economic growth.[5] The current national agreement, the *Programme for Prosperity and Fairness* (PPF), aims to substantially increase the resources allocated to social exclusion.[6] The recent UN World Summit on Social Development in Geneva identifies the need to "encourage Governments to re-evaluate, as appropriate, their national fiscal policies including progressive tax mechanisms, with the aim of reducing income inequali-

---

[3] Combat Poverty Agency (1999) *Strategic Plan 1999-20001*. Dublin: Combat Poverty Agency.

[4] Government of Ireland (1997) *Sharing in Progress: National Anti-Poverty Strategy*. Dublin: Stationery Office.

[5] Fianna Fáil and Progressive Democrats (1997) *Action Programme for the New Millennium*. Dublin: Stationery Office.

[6] Government of Ireland (2000) *Programme for Prosperity and Fairness*. Dublin: Stationery Office.

ties and promoting social equity" as part of the political declaration on proposals for further initiatives on social development.[7]

A TIMELY REPORT

Evidence from the Living in Ireland Survey[8] shows that while
consistent or severe poverty decreased between 1994 and
1997, relative income poverty increased. In other words more
households had less that 50 per cent of average income in 1997
than in 1994 and they also fell further below the relative income
poverty lines than before. This contributed to an increased gap
between rich and poor.

This report is therefore very timely as it examines this
headline finding on income poverty and tries to establish how a
growing economy could contribute to greater income inequality. It was also important to look more closely at income distribution as Ireland appeared to have a high level of income inequality relative to other EU countries. The small cluster of EU
countries with high levels of income inequality also demonstrated high levels of child poverty, another matter of serious
concern to the Agency. It is striking that, whereas in some other
countries rapid economic growth has resulted in a decline in
income inequality, Ireland's performance in this regard has
been disappointing.

The information and analysis arising from the study are crucial to the Combat Poverty Agency's ultimate objective of devising recommendations for public policy on interventions to
generate and support greater equality and a fairer redistribution of resources in our society. This will require a stronger re

---

[7] Unedited final outcome document as adopted by the Plenary of the special
session, Twenty-fourth special session of the General Assembly entitled
"World Summit for Social Development and Beyond: Achieving Social Development for all in a Globalising World", July 2000.

[8] Callan, T., R. Layte, B. Nolan, D. Watson, C.T. Whelan, J. Williams and B.
Maître (1999) *Monitoring Poverty Trends: Data from the 1997 Living in Ireland
Survey.* Dublin: ESRI, The Department of Social, Community and Family Affairs
and the Combat Poverty Agency. Preliminary findings are now also available
for 1998, which indicate a slight moderation in the relative income poverty
trend.

distribution strategy, alongside investment strategies and tax and welfare policies that complement other positive initiatives to prevent poverty. In short, addressing income inequalities needs to be a key public policy priority for the future.[9]

This report, by a research team in the Economic and Social Research Institute and NUI Maynooth who have extensive experience in the field of poverty and inequality research, is of the highest quality. It draws on data from the Living in Ireland Survey undertaken by the Institute for Eurostat, supported by the Combat Poverty Agency and the Department of Social, Community and Family Affairs, and on Household Budget Survey data from the Central Statistics Office.

The immediate policy context which the recommendations from this report will inform include the Government budgetary process, the review of the National Anti-Poverty Strategy (particularly the work of the Indexation of Welfare and Income Adequacy Working Group), commitments to social inclusion and social investment within both the *Programme for Prosperity and Fairness* and the *National Development Plan* and the strategic overview of tax and welfare policies for the next ten years currently being embarked on by the National Economic and Social Council.

Finally, this report will be complemented by a report on the *Impact of Social Spending on Inequality and Poverty*, which will be published by the Agency early in 2001. It will focus on the period covered by the last three national agreements, with a view to stimulating further public and political debate on how current fiscal and welfare policies and social spending create or reinforce inequality and poverty.

AIMS OF THE STUDY

The study looks primarily at changes in the distribution of income in Irish society between 1994 and 1997 based on data from the Living in Ireland Survey for both of those years and on the 1994/5 Household Budget Survey. In doing so it specifically:

---

[9] Combat Poverty Agency (2000) *Annual Report, 1999.* Dublin: Combat Poverty Agency.

- Places these changes in the longer term context of what has happened since 1973 through 1987 up to 1998

- Assesses how Ireland fared on the issue of income distribution relative to other EU and industrialised OECD countries

- Examines more closely the nature of those changes and the factors influencing emerging trends, e.g. inequality between particular types of households, the position of those households on the income ladder and how earnings, social welfare payments, taxation, and women's participation in the workforce impacts on these changes.

HOW INCOME IS DEFINED

This study examines household survey income data rather than tax or administrative data. These surveys collect information by way of questionnaire, on income from the following sources: employee earnings, self-employment, farming, secondary jobs, casual employment, state training or work experience schemes, social welfare transfers, child benefit, the renting of land or property, interest or dividends, retirement pensions, pensions from abroad, annuities, covenants or trusts, sick pay, strike pay, maintenance from outside the household and educational grants.

The distribution of income is described by way of income percentiles, specifically deciles, i.e. the share of total income going to the bottom 10 per cent of households, the next 10 per cent and so on up to the top 10 per cent of households; and quintiles, i.e. the share that goes to the bottom 20 per cent, the next 20 per cent and so on.

As well as looking at overall income distribution, the study also disaggregates three types of income for analysis; direct or market income, gross income which includes both market income and social welfare payments received, and finally disposable income which is the latter minus tax and insurance contributions.

Income is examined only at the household level. The issue of how that income is distributed among individuals in the household is not dealt with. It is also important to note that this study, while providing us with a comprehensive analysis of income distribution, is not a study of wealth. It does not examine the holding or accumulation of wealth in the form of profits, savings and other assets, which may be becoming increasingly significant and unequal at a time of rapid economic growth.

SUMMARY OF KEY FINDINGS

- **Overall income inequality increased between 1994 and 1998.** In the mid 1990s the bottom 10 per cent of households had about 2 per cent of total income whereas the top 10 per cent had about 27 per cent. However, between 1994 and 1998 there was a redistribution of over 1 per cent of total income away from the bottom 30 per cent of the income distribution – representing a substantial shift in a short period. The increasing inequality reflects a shift from the bottom half of the distribution to the top half, rather than to those right at the top.

- **The growth in earnings inequality continued to increase.** Dispersion in the Irish earnings distribution was relatively high by international standards in 1994 and it increased between 1987 and 1994 by more than in almost any other OECD country for which data are available. The scale of this increase in Ireland over the period showed that a rapid increase in the supply of highly educated labour and centralised wage setting were not enough to limit the growth in earnings inequality. Between 1994 and 1997, when economic growth accelerated rapidly, the increase in earnings inequality slowed although the top of the distribution did continue to move away from the middle.

- **Ireland is one of the most unequal countries in the EU.** Overall income inequality and inequality in the distribution of earnings have risen sharply during the 1980s and 1990s in a number of industrialised countries. In the mid 1990s, however, Ireland had one of the highest levels of income inequality in Europe, with the exception of Portugal and along with Spain, Portugal and the UK, was one of a group of EU countries with relatively high levels of income inequality. Based on data from the mid-1980s Ireland also ranked among the most unequal in the OECD countries. As noted earlier, this cluster of countries with high levels of income inequality is the same cluster that shows relatively high levels of child poverty.

- **Older households moved down while younger ones moved up.** The period 1994-1997 saw younger households moving up the income distribution towards the top while older ones moved down. Households headed by someone aged between 35 and 65 were fairly evenly spread throughout the income ladder. However those headed by someone under 35 were more concentrated in the top quintile by 1997 while for older households the proportion at the top declined and the numbers at the bottom rose markedly.

- **Larger families concentrated at the bottom of the income ladder.** Households with one adult with children were very heavily concentrated right at the bottom of the distribution, though less so in 1997 than in 1994. While couples with one or two children were towards the top of the distribution in both years, it is striking that those with four or more children on the other hand were very heavily concentrated at the bottom.

- **The equalising effects of social welfare transfers has diminished.** Social welfare transfers, though having an equalising effect in both 1994 and 1997 had less impact in the latter year — mainly because the numbers of households dependent on such payments declined.

- **Increasing numbers of women at work did not significantly affect income inequality.** Rapid increases in female labour force participation in the 1987-94 period have not had a significant impact on income inequality. This is largely because, despite the rapid increases in women's participation, women's earnings still only accounted for 15 per cent of total household income in 1994. The study looks at the detail of the complex changes and indicates that they may become a particularly important factor in understanding future changes.

- **Overall income inequality has fallen since 1973.** Looking back over a longer period, from 1973–1987 inequality in the distribution of household income fell markedly, with the share of the top decile down by 1.4 per cent of total income and that of the bottom quintile up by 0.9 per cent. This reflects the increasingly redistributive impact of income tax and a substantial increase in the average tax rate. From 1987 to 1994 this continued at a much slower rate. However within this overall statistic, between 1987 and 1994 wage inequality in Ireland increased substantially, even though centralised wage agreements were reintroduced in 1987 and have had a significant impact on improving the economic landscape.

UNDERSTANDING THE FINDINGS

The wider economic context for this report is one in which our wealth is clearly rising, with more people at work, an increase in the real incomes of the poor and a drop in long-term or consistent poverty and child poverty. However, relative income poverty has increased, the depth of poverty is greater, the risk of poverty for some groups is increasing and a quarter of children live in poor households.

The key lesson from this research report is that in a fast growing economy, a rising tide does not lift all boats equally. While more people are employed now than before, those at the top of the income ladder have benefited at a faster pace than those at the bottom. It is also clear that internationally Ireland fares badly on the income inequality front, and that despite undoubted advances in our general prosperity and availability of employment, we are still lagging well behind the levels of income equality that have been achieved in other modern economies in Europe or other industrialised OECD countries.

All of this raises questions about how progressive fiscal and welfare policies can be developed to ensure that this period of resource buoyancy does not lead to a more divided and more unequal society. The Combat Poverty Agency believes that it is the responsibility of government to ensure that the inequalities arising from wealth creation are controlled and ameliorated through public policy interventions. The challenge of good governance is to redress imbalances through more redistributive tax and welfare policies and investment in quality public services. Until the fair distribution of our new-found wealth is addressed, the "Celtic Tiger" will be an incomplete achievement.[10]

In addition to the national scenario, the shape and direction of government fiscal policy takes place within a European Union which now has a strengthened focus on tackling poverty and other forms of inequality through the Employment Action Plan and the Social Action Agenda, and within the context of the UN proposals on reducing income inequality which emerged from the recent World Summit and were mentioned earlier.

This presents a unique opportunity for Ireland to pursue a new model of development based *on equitable growth,* whereby the pursuit of economic growth and social cohesion are two sides of the one coin, one reinforcing the other.

POST-1998 SCENARIO

Before setting out specific policy recommendations it is worth outlining briefly the kind of trends that have occurred since 1997/98, the point to which this research report brings us. Unemployment has fallen dramatically and the economy continues its remarkably strong rate of growth — although there have been recent concerns about rising inflation and containing demand arising from supply constraints, for instance in the labour and housing markets.[11] In particular there are concerns not to overheat the economy by further fuelling inflationary pressures.

There is a fundamental link between tackling poverty and distributing income. Simulating a continuation of recent tax/welfare policies[12] it was predicted in 1999 that relative in-

---

[10] Combat Poverty Agency (1999) *From Wealth Creation to Wealth Distribution: Submission to the Minister for Social, Community and Family Affairs on Budget 2000.* Dublin: Combat Poverty Agency.

[11] McCoy, D., D. Duffy, and D. Smyth (2000) *Quarterly Economic Commentary.* Dublin: Economic and Social Research Institute.

[12] Callan, T., R. Layte, B. Nolan, D. Watson, C.T. Whelan, J. Williams and B. Maître (1999) *Monitoring Poverty Trends: Data from the 1997 Living in Ireland*

come poverty would increase by almost a half between 1994 and 2001 at the 40 per cent income poverty line. The redistributive impact of Budget 1999, while better than previous ones, primarily benefited those on middle incomes (plus 3 per cent), and despite being the most generous budget in years, gave those on the lowest incomes minimal gains. Budget 2000, largely due to tax rate reductions, was even less progressive. The result was an upward distribution of resources, with better-off households gaining up to four times more than those on low incomes. The *Programme for Prosperity and Fairness*, agreed in early 2000, (while committing considerable resources in the future to the issue of social inclusion) continued the approach of percentage pay increases along the income distribution. It also implemented the introduction of a minimum wage and contained general commitments on the future shape of income tax policy.

Given this fiscal and welfare approach since 1997/98 it would seem reasonable to assume that no significant change has been made in relation the extent of income inequality since then, certainly not in the direction of greater equality.

POLICY RECOMMENDATIONS

There are now enormous resources at the State's disposal to strategically develop public policy interventions that will control income inequalities arising from a growing economy and prevent the continuation of a more divided society as we move into the 21st century. To date, public policy has relied too heavily on job creation alone to solve the problems of inequality, social exclusion and poverty.

A more strategic and planned approach is required. Such a strategic approach needs to focus on five broad public policy interventions.

- Firstly, establishing adequate welfare payments and child benefit rates and ensuring, in a transparent way, that the value of those payments are protected.

Survey. Dublin: ESRI, The Department of Social, Community and Family Affairs and the Combat Poverty Agency.

- Secondly, eliminating welfare and poverty traps thereby easing the transition to work for those who can take up employment, or are already in low paid employment, and investing in human capital through training and education for this group.

- Thirdly, removing the tax burden on the low paid over time by taking those on the minimum wage out of the tax net and creating a more progressive tax system by concentrating on completing the move to tax credits and increasing tax allowances (or credits) rather than cutting tax rates.

- Fourthly, placing a more explicit emphasis on those on the lowest wages in the centralised pay bargaining process.

- Fifthly, strategic investment in public services, particularly health, housing, education, childcare and transport.

THE ANNUAL BUDGET

To avoid the emergence of a more divided society, a budgetary strategy which re-balances the tax and welfare package in favour of those on low incomes and on welfare is required. The distribution of resources should not negatively impact on work incentives, given the importance of work as a route out of poverty.

The Government, however, should not rely entirely on rising employment to address growing inequalities. Firstly, because there is evidence that one factor contributing to a slow down in labour force growth in Ireland is that potential labour supply is reaching a limit,[13] and secondly, because employment may not be an option for a proportion of those on the lowest incomes (for instance those who are ill or disabled, mothers choosing to stay at home while their children are young, or those who are retired). While worklessness is still a cause of poverty, particularly for families with children, research from

---

[13] Mc Coy, D., D. Duffy and D. Smyth (2000) *Quarterly Economic Commentary.* Dublin: Economic and Social Research Institute.

the UK, for example, shows that only half of poor families have someone available to enter employment.[14]

Budget analyses conducted by the Agency in recent years using the SWITCH model (a micro-simulation model demonstrating the effects of tax and welfare changes across the income distribution) have shown how the distributional benefits have been in favour of those on middle or higher incomes. The key mechanism for sharing our growing wealth is the annual Budget. The challenge for future budgets is to reverse the pattern to date and ensure that tax and welfare reforms redistribute resources in favour of the least well-off in society.

In this regard the Agency recommends the more rigorous application of poverty-proofing procedures to budget proposals in the future. This commitment is made in the *Programme for Prosperity and Fairness*, particularly around budget taxation proposals.

THE NATIONAL ANTI-POVERTY STRATEGY (NAPS)

While consistent poverty (based on income poverty and deprivation measures combined) is falling, relative income poverty has been increasing. The increase in relative income poverty, and the widening of the gap between rich and poor, has implications for NAPS in the longer term. The challenge for NAPS in the current, benign macro-economic environment is to tackle both the remaining consistently poor and to address the "broader maldistribution of income".[15]

A review of NAPS agreed under the PPF includes the establishment of an Indexation and Income Adequacy Working Group, which will examine the issue of relative income poverty and the adequacy of welfare payments. In the context of the work of this Working Group, specific consideration should be given to how our growing income inequality can be curtailed

---

[14] Aber, L. (2000) *The Impact of Child Poverty on Children's Well-Being*. Paper to the Combat Poverty Agency Conference on Child Poverty, July 2000. Dublin: Combat Poverty Agency.

[15] Johnston, H. and T. O'Brien (2000) *Planning for a More Inclusive Society: An Initial Assessment of the National Anti-Poverty Strategy*. Dublin: Combat Poverty Agency.

and the gap between rich and poor narrowed through the NAPS strategy and its targets.

Three proposals for consideration in the light of the review of NAPS are as follows:

- Introduce a relative income poverty reduction target to complement and strengthen existing targets.[16]

- Introduce a NAPS target for reducing income inequality. The most commonly used measure of income inequality is the Gini Coefficient. This study shows that Ireland has a Gini Coefficient above the EU average, and well above that found in countries such as Denmark and the Netherlands.

- Integrate an income inequality dimension into the poverty proofing process.

SOCIAL WELFARE

Adequacy and Indexation

In relation to the role of social welfare this research raises two specific but related issues: establishing an adequate welfare payment; and determining in a transparent way how rates can be indexed so as to maintain the relative value of payments. Adequacy and indexation are critical issues that have been identified in the PPF to be examined by a working group under the terms of that agreement. The research highlights the urgency of doing this.

In recent years the Agency has recommended that payments be raised in line with earnings, as fast rising earnings have outpaced both inflation and the rate of welfare increases, leaving those on welfare behind. The failure to link welfare payments to increases in earnings means that those outside the labour market find their situation relatively disimproved, thus contributing to the growing gap between rich and poor.

---

[16] See, for example, National Economic and Social Forum (2000) *The National Anti-Poverty Strategy*. Forum Opinion No. 8. Dublin: National Economic and Social Forum.

The Agency recommendation that welfare increases be indexed to rising earnings was predicated on low rates of inflation, which have been a feature of Irish economic recovery. However we have just experienced a sharp rise in price inflation, which is now not only outstripping welfare increases but also wage increases agreed in the *Programme for Prosperity and Fairness* (2000).[17]

Both price inflation and rising earnings contribute to the pattern of consumer norms and expectations and the resulting "standard of living". There is therefore an argument for indexation to be linked to either of these, depending on which is higher, in order to offer effective protection to the relative value of welfare payments. This is certainly a complex issue, which requires immediate attention in the current economic and policy context.

Finally, in the absence of an integrated child income support policy, the indexation of welfare rates should also apply to child dependent allowances.

Transitions to Work

There is a continued need to ease the transition from welfare to work by addressing remaining disincentives for those taking up work. A strengthened Child Benefit, including a "top-up" to cover childcare costs, would play a significant role in this regard. This was a central policy recommendation from the Agency in its recent submission to the Government on the National Children's Strategy.[18]

A reformed child income policy should incorporate an enhanced universal benefit for all children, set at a given proportion of the total costs of raising a child. The Agency suggests that this proportion should be in the region of two-thirds of the total costs, which is currently the equivalent of £25 per child per week. In addition, the provision of a universal childcare

---

[17] It is noted that this impact on wages may not follow through completely to net pay, depending on the nature of tax improvements that complement wage increases.

[18] Combat Poverty Agency (2000) *A Better Future for Children: Eliminating Poverty, Promoting Equality. Submission to the National children's Strategy.* Dublin: Combat Poverty Agency.

subsidy (funded by restricting the transferability of tax bands between married couples) would support all families with children, not just those liable for tax. This could play an important role in supporting parents making the transition from welfare to full or part-time work.

Reform of the tax system requires action on a number of fronts: maintaining tax revenue (as a proportion of GNP/GDP) as a means of supporting a more progressive and inclusive society, payment of taxes, progressivity of personal income tax, and broadening the tax base.

Maintaining Tax Revenue

Working towards a more progressive tax system is important to ensure fairness, while maintaining tax revenue at a level to fund much needed public service expenditure is also important. Recent budget decisions (e.g. cutting the higher rate of tax) may compound rather than improve the public service inadequacies and infrastructural bottlenecks which are being highlighted increasingly as the two chief obstacles to Irish economic sustainability.

Clearly there are limits to the extent to which tax rates can be cut, if we are to achieve greater social inclusion through public policy. At European level, examining taxation in the 15 EU countries, tax revenue as a percentage of GDP increased from 40.7 per cent in 1987 to 41.5 per cent in 1997. In contrast, over the same period the ratio of tax revenue to GDP in Ireland fell from 37.4 per cent to 32.8 per cent.[19] Consideration could be given to setting a target for fiscal policy to move toward the EU average ratio of tax/GDP(or GNP).

European economies with greater levels of income equality tend also to have above average tax/GDP ratios. Cuts in the tax rates restrict the resources available to the state for public policy interventions to achieve greater equality between citizens. Evidence from opinion surveys suggests public support for the

---

[19] Organisation for Economic Co-Operation and Development (1999) *Revenue Statistics.* Paris: OECD. For further analysis see "Inequality in the New Irish Economy", chapter by Colm O'Reardon from the forthcoming book on Social Spending and Inequality from the Combat Poverty Agency.

notion that taxation is a form of social solidarity. However, the perception that some can get away with tax evasion more easily than others needs to be dealt with and counteracted. The public needs to be confident that the tax system is fair, that revenue is collected equitably and that resources will be reinvested in public services for the common good.

Payment of Taxes

It is a core principle of a socially cohesive society that all members pay their fair share of taxes and claim only their legitimate entitlements. Recent behaviour, as revealed by the investigations of the Public Accounts Committee, has cast a cloud over this principle. Every effort should be made to remedy the perception that those with large amounts of wealth can "get away with" tax evasion whereas those on low and middle incomes pay automatically through the PAYE system.

More Progressive Income Tax System

Moves toward a more progressive income tax system include:

- Increasing standardised personal and PAYE allowances (or tax credits). This is a fairer approach to tax reform as it benefits all taxpayers equally and it improves work incentives for low earners. This should work progressively towards the objective of taking everyone on the minimum wage out of the tax net.

- No further cuts in the top rate of tax. The focus on allowances means that there should be no change in either the tax bands or the tax rates.

- Restricting the transferability of tax bands between married couples — on the basis that this is an ineffective subvention for children — and investing revenue saved in improved Child Benefit.

Broadening the Tax Base

The Government has indicated its intention to reduce corporation tax to 12.5 per cent while profits in this sector are spiralling. The Agency believes that the long-term implications of this reduction should be reconsidered. Alternatively the introduction of a clawback tax, especially in non-traded sectors might be examined. The Agency also supports the introduction of environmental and other forms of "polluter-pays" taxes.

THE PROBLEM OF LOW PAY

The principal policy instrument designed to deal with the problem of low pay is the national minimum wage, which was introduced in 2000. It is, as yet, too early to assess the impact of this intervention. However, it is clear that the minimum wage legislation is not a panacea for low pay and resulting inequality.[20] Recent poverty figures show that the numbers in work and under the poverty line, while still relatively small, doubled between 1994 and 1997.[21] The role of childcare support, the elimination of poverty traps and the value of in-work supports are important policy interventions to tackle the problem of low pay.

As with social welfare payments, the issue of how the minimum wage will be uprated is very important. The recommended rate will need to be subject to annual review and uprating so that the position of low paid workers does not fall behind average earnings in relative terms. It is also important that the implementation of the minimum wage is monitored effectively and that adequate public resources for this monitoring are provided.

However, neither eliminating poverty traps nor uprating the minimum wage will deal with the question of how low paid workers can be supported to progress within the labour market, advance their skills and qualifications and achieve long-term income security through work. This will require an investment in human capital through the provision of education and training supports to those in low paid work.

---

[20] For more detail see the Combat Poverty Agency submission to the Commission on the National Minimum Wage, December 1997.

[21] Callan, T., R. Layte, B. Nolan, D. Watson, C.T. Whelan, J. Williams and B. Maître (1999) *Monitoring Poverty Trends: Data from the 1997 Living in Ireland Survey.* Dublin: ESRI, The Department of Social, Community and Family Affairs and the Combat Poverty Agency. Preliminary figures for 1998 indicate that this trend has not been maintained in 1998.

THE ROLE OF CENTRALISED PAY BARGAINING

Despite ten years of centralised pay bargaining earnings dispersion has continued to widen. It is not clear why this is the case. Centralised pay bargaining has been credited with underpinning wage moderation and the recovery of the Irish economy, even though earnings dispersion has continued to occur in this context. There is scope now for examining how national wage agreements can more explicitly address the needs of the low paid in the future, through a combination of pay, taxation packages and other benefits. This may require a reappraisal of the traditional approach of percentage pay increases across the board.

While this examination will help focus on the problem of low pay, it will not deal with continuing earnings dispersion which arises from the movement in earnings of those outside the control of centralised pay bargaining, i.e. self-employed professionals or private sector multinational company employees.

FURTHER RESEARCH

There are two areas for further research highlighted by this report. Firstly, the extent and distribution of wealth in our society, and secondly, the issue of how income is distributed within households. Both of these have been the subject of studies by the Agency[22] in the early 1990s, but need to be revisited in what is now a very different context, both from the point of view of the economy and the policy environment.

There is increasing evidence that there has recently been a "dramatic shift in income shares from labour to capital".[23] In other words, the proportion of national income from profits has increased and the proportion of national income from wages has reduced dramatically over the last decade. The extent of wealth holdings is therefore more relevant than ever before to our understanding of inequality *per se*. While it is notoriously

---

[22] Rottman, D. (1994) *Income Distribution Within Households*. Dublin: Combat Poverty Agency, and Nolan, B. (1991) *The Wealth of Irish Households*. Dublin: Combat Poverty Agency.

[23] Lane, P. (1998) *Profits and Wages in Ireland: 1987-1996*. Trinity Economic Papers, Technical Paper No. 14.

difficult to obtain information on wealth it is important to reflect on how a more rigorous knowledge and understanding of it could contribute to our understanding of how to achieve greater equality and social inclusion.

There have been a number of efforts in recent years to examine more closely how income is distributed within households and this report underlines how important it is to revisit the issue. In this regard, the Agency has now commissioned a report on the intra-household allocation of resources, which will be available in 2001.

Finally the Agency would like to acknowledge and thank the research team at the ESRI and NUI Maynooth who undertook this study: Brian Nolan, Bertrand Maître, Donal O'Neill and Olive Sweetman. The research is of the highest standard and the Combat Poverty Agency is very grateful for this excellent report and the dedicated attention to detail throughout.

Combat Poverty Agency
November 2000

Executive Summary

Overall income inequality and inequality in the distribution of earnings have risen sharply during the 1980s and 1990s in a number of industrialised countries, giving rise to widespread concern about the factors at work and the societal implications. This makes it particularly important to know how the distribution of income in Ireland has been changing over time, how it compares with other countries, and what factors contribute to explaining Ireland's particular experience.

This study first uses data from the Living in Ireland surveys carried out by the Economic and Social Research Institute to provide a picture of the distribution of household income in Ireland in the 1990s. A key finding is that there was a marked shift in the disposable income distribution away from the bottom 30 per cent over the period from 1994 to 1998. The share going to the bottom 30 per cent of households declined by almost one and a half per cent of total income (adjusted for differences in household size and composition). The distribution among households of income coming directly from the market did not become more unequal over the period; instead, an important factor was that the equalising effect of social welfare transfers declined. Increases in income share were seen over the top half of the distribution, rather than concentrated right at the top. There was also some change in the composition of both top and bottom income groups, with younger households moving up and older ones moving down.

Over the period from 1973-87, on the other hand, inequality in the distribution of disposable household income had fallen markedly, with the share of the bottom quintile up by almost 1 per cent of total income and the share of the top decile falling. This was partly because the redistributive impact of income tax and employees' social insurance contributions increased, reflecting both increasing progressivity and a very substantial rise in the average tax rate. From 1987 to 1994 this continued but at a much slower rate, helping to explain the greater stability in the shape of the income distribution over those years.

Turning to international comparisons, data from the European Community Household Panel Survey shows Ireland to have one of the more unequal income distributions in the EU in the mid-1990s. Ireland is one of a group of EU countries – the others being the UK, Greece and Spain - with relatively high inequality, though not as high as Portugal. A fairly widespread, though not universal, trend towards increased inequality in the period from the mid-1980s to the mid-1990s was found in a recent OECD comparative study. The most notable common underlying feature was that the share of earnings going to the lower income groups among the working population decreased in all the countries covered in the study.

Data from the ESRI household surveys are also used to examine the distribution of earnings among Irish employees. The dispersion in earnings is found to be relatively high by international standards in 1994, having increased relatively rapidly from 1987. Between 1994 and 1997, when Irish economic growth accelerated rapidly, the increase in earnings inequality slowed although the top of the distribution continued to move away from the middle.

The participation of married women in the paid labour force has been increasing rapidly in Ireland, so their wages have been accounting for a growing proportion of household income. Elsewhere, this has been seen to increase household income inequality. That does not appear to have been the case for Ireland between 1987 and 1994, mostly because increases in female employment rates over that period were greatest among wives married to husbands with relatively low earnings.

Chapter 1

Introduction

Brian Nolan

An accurate picture of the distribution of income, and an adequate grasp of how it comes about, is crucial for policy formation and for understanding the society in which we live. Recent international research has highlighted the fact that both overall income inequality and inequality in the distribution of earnings have risen sharply during the 1980s and 1990s in a number of industrialised countries, notably the UK and the USA. This makes it particularly important to know how the distribution of income in Ireland has been changing over time, how it compares with other countries, and what factors contribute to explaining Ireland's particular experience. The aim of this study is to address these issues, using household survey data.

These data allow us to first provide a picture of the distribution of household income in Ireland in the 1990s, so one can both see what the shape of that distribution is and how it has been changing recently. This distribution may be compared with similar figures for 1987 and earlier years, to assess trends over a longer period. These results for Ireland can also be compared with estimates for other countries, so that both Ireland's current distribution and trends over time can be placed in comparative perspective. Finally, the survey data for Ireland allow us to explore the factors underlying the distribution, notably the relationship between the overall household income distribution and the distribution of earnings among individual earners.

The study is structured as follows. Chapter 2 describes the survey data on which the study relies and how income and its distribution are measured. Chapter 3 examines the distribution of household income in Ireland in the 1990s. Chapter 4 makes use of data from earlier surveys to analyse how the distribution of income in Ireland changed between 1987 and 1994, and also to examine longer-term trends in the income distribution back to 1973. Chapter 5 focuses on how the level of inequality in the distribution of household income in Ireland compares with other countries. Chapter 6 turns to the distribution of earnings, the most important source of income, and how this evolved in Ireland over the decade from 1987. Chapter 7 then looks at the relationship between the earnings distribution and the overall distribution of income among households, focusing in particular on the way in which the earnings of husbands and their wives are related, and how that influences the household income distribution. Finally, Chapter 8 brings together the main findings.

Chapter 2

Measuring the Distribution of Income in Ireland

Brian Nolan

2.1 INTRODUCTION

Before one can examine empirical evidence about the distribution of income, it is essential to have an understanding of the way incomes, their distribution, and the extent of inequality are measured. The aim of this chapter is to describe the data on which this study relies, and outline how income and its distribution are to be measured. Section 2.2 focuses on the description of the household surveys to be employed and the information they obtain on income. Section 2.3 outlines methodological issues which arise in measuring the distribution of income and the extent of income inequality, and the approaches to be adopted in this study.

2.2 MEASURING THE DISTRIBUTION OF INCOME: DATA AND PREVIOUS RESEARCH

Studies of the distribution of income in Ireland rely on household surveys rather than administrative tax/social security records to provide the database. (See Nolan, 1978 for a discussion of the use of survey versus administrative data on income distribution in the Irish case, and Callan, 1991a, for a discussion of survey and Revenue Commissioners income data). In this study we rely on data from two sets of large-scale household surveys. The first comprises the survey carried out by the ESRI in 1987,

and the longitudinal survey initiated in 1994. The 1987 Survey
of Income Distribution, Poverty and Use of State Services is described in detail in Callan, Nolan *et al.*, 1989, the 1994 Living in
Ireland Survey is described in Callan *et al.*, 1996, and Callan *et
al.*, 1999 describes the 1997 Living in Ireland Survey. These
surveys have already provided the foundation on which an extensive programme of research on the extent and nature of
poverty, and a wide range of related topics, has been based
(see Nolan and Callan, 1994; Callan *et al.*, 1996; Callan *et al.*,
1999). The 1987 survey has also provided data for Ireland for
the Luxembourg Income Study database, employed in the recent comprehensive comparative study of income distribution
in OECD countries by Atkinson, Rainwater and Smeeding
(1995).

The other set of surveys from which estimates of the income
distribution can be derived is the Household Budget Survey
(HBS) carried out by the Central Statistics Office. As its name
indicates this is primarily an expenditure survey, but it contains
detailed income data and serves as an invaluable source for
analysis of the income distribution. The HBS has been carried
out in 1973, 1980, 1987 and 1994/95, with results from the most
recent survey (1999/2000) not yet available. A detailed description of the HBS is given in Murphy (1984). The income information obtained in the ESRI surveys and in the HBS is very
similar, although differences in exact timing between the latest
two HBS surveys and the ESRI 1987 and 1994 surveys have to be
taken into account in making comparisons. The micro-data
tapes for the 1987 and 1994/95 HBS (suitably anonymised) have
now been released by the CSO to researchers for the first time,
and are analysed here. We also make use of published results
from the 1973 and 1980 HBS to provide a longer perspective on
trends in income inequality back to the early 1970s.

Most previous research on the distribution of income in Ireland has been based on the Household Budget Surveys and the
1987 and 1994 ESRI surveys. Nolan (1978) used the published
results from the 1973 HBS to provide the first picture of the
overall distribution of income among Irish households. Murphy
(1984, 1985) explored in greater detail the distribution in the
1973 and 1980 HBS, based on analysis of the micro-data from

within the CSO. Rottman and Reidy (1988) also used data provided by the CSO from the 1973 and 1980 HBS. Callan and Nolan (1997) looked at trends in inequality in the household income distribution in the 1973, 1980 and 1987 HBS, based on these previous studies for 1973 and 1980 and data supplied by the CSO from the 1987 HBS. Data on household incomes from the 1987 ESRI survey was lodged with the Luxembourg Income Study database, and as already noted was used in the recent comprehensive comparative study of income distribution in OECD countries by Atkinson, Rainwater and Smeeding (1995). Callan and Nolan (1999) analysed trends up to the 1994 Living in Ireland Survey, while O'Neill and Sweetman (1998) compared the 1987 and 1994/95 HBS. The availability of these micro-datasets, together with data from later waves of the ESRI's Living in Ireland Survey, opens up new possibilities for exploring the structure of the income distribution and trends in income inequality in Ireland.

Detailed descriptions of the ESRI and HBS surveys have been given elsewhere, but it is important to set out here the nature of the income measures and the information obtained in the surveys to construct them. The questionnaires collected information on income from the following sources: employee earnings, self-employment, farming, secondary jobs, casual employment, State training or work experience schemes, Social Welfare transfers by scheme, Child Benefit, the renting of land or property, interest or dividends, retirement pensions, pensions from abroad, annuities, covenants or trusts, sick pay from an employer, trade union strike or sick pay, private or charitable maintenance from outside the household (including alimony payments), and educational grants.

The time period covered by the income information is important. The ESRI surveys and Household Budget Survey adopt the same approach, recording details for most sources of income, such as earnings, Social Welfare transfers, and private pensions, in respect of the amount received in the current pay period (week, fortnight, month, etc.). A longer reference period was used for certain other income sources, because it would not be very meaningful to collect details on current weekly or monthly receipts in respect of income from self-employment, farming, property rental or investment income. In respect of these income sources details were recorded on the basis of the most recently available annual figures, converted to a weekly average for the construction of the income measures. A different approach is followed in the European Community Household Panel Survey (ECHP), in which an annual accounting period is adopted throughout. Since the ESRI Living in Ireland surveys comprised the Irish element of the ECHP, they also obtained that annual income data, along with current receipts. We defer discussion of the ECHP and its annual income measure until Chapter 5, concentrating until then on current income as measured in the ESRI surveys and the HBS.

Collecting information on income from farming poses special problems and here there were some differences in methodology and timing between the ESRI surveys and the HBS. In the ESRI surveys, farm income in the previous calendar year was estimated indirectly on the basis of information on output and stocking levels collected in an additional questionnaire administered to farm households, in conjunction with soil type and detailed family farm income coefficients provided by Teagasc. In the HBS for both 1987 and 1994, the CSO was able to integrate a sample of farm households from the National Farm Survey conducted by Teagasc, which involves maintenance of annual farm accounts, and these households were also administered the standard HBS questionnaire. Interviews for the 1994-95 HBS were carried out between May 1994 and July 1995, so in some instances farm income referred to 1994.

The income details collected allow one to derive various income concepts. The aggregate income measures employed in this study are *direct or market income*, *gross income* (market income plus social welfare payments received) and *disposable income* (gross income less income tax and employees' social security contributions).[1] These income definitions employed in

---

[1] Note that for an employee this may not be the same as take-home pay, which will be net of a range of other deductions, including superannuation contributions, Trade Union subscriptions, life insurance premia, VHI subscriptions, regular savings or mortgage repayments deducted by the employer at source.

the ESRI surveys are in line with those adopted by the CSO in the Household Budget Survey, and allow both sources of data to be used on a consistent basis.

The final point to be made about the household surveys on which Irish income distribution studies rely is that they of course provide only samples from the population, unlike for example administrative data on tax and social welfare which cover all those paying tax or receiving transfers. The representativeness of such samples vis-a-vis the overall population must therefore be a constant concern. Complex weighting schemes are employed in both the ESRI surveys and the HBS in order to align the samples with external information on for example the overall age distribution, the distribution of households across urban versus rural areas, and social class composition. In the case of the Living in Ireland Surveys an extra dimension is involved because in a longitudinal survey, following the same people from year to year, not everyone from the initial sample can be successfully interviewed in subsequent years — there is attrition from the sample. The reweighting scheme employed takes this into account and seeks to compensate for any observed concentration of attrition among specific groups. Results such as those presented here, drawn from household surveys, must none the less be seen as estimates subject to error. Statistical methods for assessing the likely bounds on such error in the case of income inequality measures have been developing significantly in recent years and have an important role to play, though longitudinal datasets by their nature still pose particular problems.

2.3 MEASURING THE DISTRIBUTION OF INCOME: METHODOLOGY

A range of methodological issues has to be addressed in measuring the distribution of income. Here our aim is not to provide a comprehensive treatment of these issues, but rather to note the key ones and state clearly the approaches followed here. (For in-depth discussion on the measurement of income inequality see for example Atkinson, Rainwater and Smeeding, 1995; Cowell, 1995; Jenkins 1991).

While the ultimate source of concern is the welfare of the individual, the income accruing to each individual is not a satisfactory measure of their command over resources because income is generally shared among individuals in a given family or broader household. The extent to which income is actually shared within the household so as to equalise living standards is an empirical question which has received some attention (see for example Lundberg, Pollak and Wales, 1997; Cantillon and Nolan, 1998; 2000) but is particularly difficult to address. It is not pursued here, where we follow the conventional approach of employing the household as the income recipient unit.[2]

Since a given income will provide a different living standard to the individuals in a large versus a small household, or one comprising adults rather than mostly children, income has to be adjusted for differences in household size and composition. Equivalence scales are intended to make such an adjustment, with actual household income being divided by the number of equivalent adults in the household to produce equivalent or equivalised income. Equivalence scales may take only household size into account, or they may incorporate both the number and age of household members. A very wide range of scales is employed within and across countries, and there is no consensus as to which set of scales or methodologies for estimating them is most satisfactory or appropriate. Studies such as Buhman *et al.* (1988) and Coulter, Cowell and Jenkins (1992) have shown the extent to which the equivalence scale employed can affect the measured income distribution (even when only size is being taken into account).

It is therefore necessary to assess the sensitivity of the results to variation in the equivalence scale employed. Here we do this by using five different equivalence scales. The first is one of the scales which has been employed in analysis of poverty in the ESRI surveys, corresponding to the scales implicit in

---

[2] The household is defined in the ECHP as comprising "either one person living alone or a group of persons, not necessarily related, living at the same address with common housekeeping — i.e. sharing a meal on most days or sharing a living or sitting room" (Eurostat 1999, p. 25). The CSO employ a similar definition in the Household Budget Survey.

Irish social welfare rates in the late 1980s. This attributes a value of 1 to the household head, 0.66 to each other adult, and 0.33 to each child in the household. The second scale has been widely used in the UK, and is closer to the values for additional adults towards which Irish social welfare rates have moved in recent years: this attributes a value of 0.6 to each additional adult and 0.4 to each child. The three other sets of scales have been commonly employed in cross-country income distribution and poverty studies. One is the square root of household size, without distinguishing between adults and children (see for example, Atkinson, Rainwater and Smeeding, 1995). The other two are widely known as the OECD and the "modified OECD" scales (see for example Hagenaars, De Vos and Zaidi, 1994). Where the first adult in the household is given a value of 1, under the OECD scale each other adult is attributed a value of 0.7 and each child is attributed a value of 0.5. With the modified OECD scale, each adult is attributed a value of 0.5 and each child 0.3. As in Hagenaars *et al.*, we take adult here to mean age 14 years or over.

A further issue is whether one focuses on the distribution of income or poverty among households, which attributes each household equal weight in the analysis, or on the distribution among individuals. As noted by Atkinson, Rainwater and Smeeding, it makes sense to treat each household as a single unit (i.e. to apply household weights) if no adjustment is made to income for household size. When equivalent income is used, though, person weights seem more appropriate. This is achieved by weighting each household in the analysis by the number of persons it contains. However, much of the previous research on the Irish income distribution refers to the distribution among households, and it is only on this basis that results from the 1973 and 1980 Household Budget Surveys are available. For that reason we will be dealing with the distribution among households at some points, and the distribution among persons at others, in the present study.

The distribution of income among households and/or persons may be portrayed and summarised in a number of different ways. Here we generally rank cases by income and then derive decile shares — the share of total income going to the bottom 10 per cent, the next per cent, . . . top 10 per cent. In looking at the earnings distribution we follow conventional practice and the deciles or quartiles of the distribution as percentages of the median — the earnings at the 10th percentile point, 25th percentile . . . 90th percentile point as percentages of median earnings. In addition, various summary measures of inequality are employed here. These are the Gini coefficient, Theil's entropy measure, the coefficient of variation, the mean logarithmic deviation, the Atkinson inequality measure with a coefficient (i.e. inequality aversion parameter) of 0.5 and 1.0, and the ratio of the top to the bottom decile, P^{90}/P^{10}. Such measures, designed to summarise the degree to which incomes are concentrated, are commonly used in the study of income inequality. Since some inequality measures put most weight on income differences in different parts of the distribution to others, all such measures will not always display the same trends, so it is worth looking at more than one. In addition, some measures are more suitable than others for specific types of analysis, in particular decomposition into sub-groups or income sources. We will not attempt to review here their derivation and properties, on which there is an extensive literature: a comprehensive description is given in e.g. Cowell (1995).

Summary measures represent one approach to capturing and comparing the level of inequality in different income distributions. Lorenz curves, on the other hand, show the whole distribution in graphical form. As illustrated in Figure 2.1, this shows the share of total income going to the bottom x per cent of the distribution, where x goes from 0 to 100 per cent. Where the Lorenz curve for one distribution lies above that for another distribution at all points, this means that the bottom x per cent of the first distribution has a higher share than in the second distribution no matter which value we choose for x. For distributions with the same mean income, it has been shown that this means that the first distribution can be taken to have a higher level of what economists term "social welfare", for quite a wide variety of social welfare functions. Where the Lorenz curves intersect, on the other hand, no such unambiguous ranking of the distributions is available — it will depend on the weight we assign to different parts of the distribution (see Cowell, 1995).

Figure 2.1: Lorenz Curve for Income

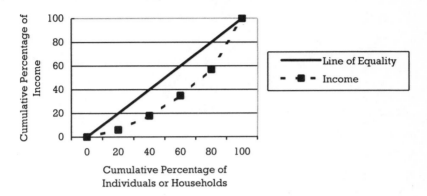

What about where the two distributions have different levels of mean income? Generalised Lorenz curves provide a convenient way of incorporating information about average living standards and inequality into the comparison of the level of social welfare yielded by different distributions. This involves plotting cumulative mean incomes (instead of cumulative income shares in standard Lorenz curves) against cumulative population shares (see Shorrocks, 1983; Jenkins, 1991). Once again, unambiguous rankings will only be available in certain circumstances, but the value of the approach is precisely in allowing us to identify when that occurs.

2.4 CONCLUSIONS

This chapter has outlined the data and methods to be employed in measuring the distribution of income in this study. The study relies on data from large-scale household surveys carried out by the ESRI and the CSO. The methodological choices faced in such a study include the choice of income recipient unit, how best to adjust income for the size and composition of the household, and how best to present and summarise the shape of the income distribution. We go on in the next chapter to use these methods to analyse the distribution of income in Ireland in the 1990s.

Chapter 3

The Distribution of Income in Ireland in the 1990s

Brian Nolan and Bertrand Maître

3.1 INTRODUCTION

In this chapter we look at the distribution of income among Irish
households and persons in the 1990s. We use for this purpose
data from the Living in Ireland Survey, which as we saw in the
last chapter was initiated in 1994. We have been able to analyse
in some depth income data from that first wave and from the
fourth wave of the survey, carried out in 1997. Data from the
1998 wave of the survey, coming on stream as this study was
completed, allowed us to also include some initial results for
that year. This chapter concentrates on the broad pattern of income distribution and recent changes as revealed by these
surveys. In the next chapter we make use of the 1987 ESRI
household survey and the CSO's Household Budget Surveys to
assess trends from 1987 to 1994 and over a longer period back
to 1973.[1]

We first look in Section 3.2 at the distribution of market,
gross and disposable income among households in 1994 and
1997, without any adjustment for differences in household size
and composition. Section 3.3 then looks at the shape of the distribution when adjustment for such differences has been made

---

[1] In doing so we also compare the results of the Living in Ireland Survey 1994
with the 1994/95 HBS; for this chapter we confine our attention here to the
Living in Ireland Surveys.

by equivalisation, using alternative equivalence scales. The distributions of equivalised household income among households and among persons are also compared. Section 3.4 analyses the components of change in the distribution between 1994 and 1997. Section 3.5 examines where different types of household tend to be located in the distribution. Section 3.6 presents some initial results for 1998. Finally, Section 3.7 summarises the main findings of the chapter.

3.2 THE DISTRIBUTION OF DISPOSABLE INCOME AMONG HOUSEHOLDS IN 1994 AND 1997

We begin by examining the distribution of disposable income – the income concept which has the most direct relevance for ability to spend — among households in the 1994 and 1997 Living in Ireland Surveys (LII). Table 3.1 shows the share in total income going to each decile. We see that in each year the bottom 10 per cent of households had about 2 per cent of total income, while the top 10 per cent had about one-quarter of the total. In broad terms a similar shape for the income distribution is seen in other industrialised countries, and the comparison with other EU and OECD countries presented in Chapter 5 will help to put Ireland's distribution in perspective. For the present, though, we concentrate on the Irish pattern and on how it has been changing between 1994 and 1997.

Two inequality measures designed to summarise the degree to which incomes are concentrated are also shown in Table 3.1, namely the Gini and Theil measures. As mentioned in the previous chapter, different inequality measures put most weight on income differences in different parts of the distribution, and all such measures will not always display the same trends, so it is worth looking at more than one. We see from the table that these summary measures calculated for disposable income suggest little difference in the level of inequality between the 1994 and 1997 surveys. However, looking at the decile shares we see that this overall stability masks the fact that there was a slight shift away from both the bottom and the top of the distribution, with those in the middle gaining.

Table 3.1: Decile Shares and Summary Inequality Measures, Disposable Income among Irish Households, 1994 and 1997 Living in Ireland Surveys

	Share in Total Disposable Income (%)	
Decile	*1994 LII*	*1997 LII*
Bottom	2.3	2.1
2	3.3	3.3
3	4.6	4.5
4	6.0	6.0
5	7.5	7.7
6	9.1	9.5
7	11.1	11.2
8	13.5	13.4
9	16.5	16.5
Top	26.4	25.8
All	100.0	100.0
Inequality Measure		
Gini	0.377	0.373
Theil	0.237	0.236

As well as shares, it is worth stating the actual income levels required to bring one into for example, the top 10 per cent of the distribution, and what constitutes an "average" income. In 1997, the median point in the disposable income distribution among households — the point which splits the distribution exactly in two — was about £290 per week or £15,100 per annum. The income cut-off for the top decile — the lowest income which would bring a household into the top 10 per cent — was about £630 per week or £32,700 per year. The income below which a household would be in the bottom 10 per cent, on the other hand, was about £84 per week or £4,400 per year. No account has been taken so far of differences in household size and composition, which obviously affect the living standard one can reach on these various income levels. It is instructive none the less to know what these absolute figures are, since there may be widespread misper-

ception of, for example, how high an income is required to lo-
cate one in the top ranges of the distribution.

We now turn to the distribution of income from the market,
and market income plus cash transfers, and see how these
compare with disposable income. Table 3.2 presents decile
shares in direct (market), gross and disposable income among
households in the 1994 and 1997 LII surveys. Unsurprisingly, in
each year the distribution of market income is very much more
unequal than that of gross or disposable income: the bottom 30
per cent of the distribution has virtually no income from the
market, while the top 10 per cent has about one-third of the total. State cash transfers bring about a substantial change in the
shape of the distribution, with the share of the bottom 30 per
cent of households rising to about 8 per cent of total income,
and the share of the top deciles falling significantly. The difference between gross income shares and those for disposable
income is less marked, but the latter does have higher shares at
the bottom and lower ones at the top: income tax and employee's social insurance contributions do move the distribution further in the direction of greater equality.

This is reflected in the Gini and Theil coefficients for these
distributions. Going from direct to gross income, State cash
transfers reduced the Gini coefficient by about one-quarter in
1994. Going from gross to disposable income, direct tax reduced the Gini by a further 10 per cent in that year. As is commonly the case in industrialised countries, both cash transfers
and direct tax thus have an equalising impact on the shape of
the income distribution, with the effect of transfers being substantially more pronounced.

We can also see from Table 3.2 that for market income, inequality did not in fact increase between 1994 and 1997. Both the
Gini and Theil coefficients suggest that inequality actually fell
for direct income between 1994 and 1997. For gross income, on
the other hand, there was little change in the summary measures. This is illustrated by the fact that in 1997 these transfers
reduced the Gini coefficient by 22 per cent, compared with 25
per cent in 1994. The relationship between gross and disposable income was broadly unchanged from 1994 to 1997. De-
creasing inequality in market income was thus offset by the di-

minishing impact of State cash transfers in reducing inequality, leaving little change in the disposable income distribution.

Table 3.2: Decile Shares for Direct and Gross Income among Households, 1994 and 1997 LII Surveys

Decile	Share in Total Income (%)					
	Direct		Gross		Disposable	
	1994	1997	1994	1997	1994	1997
Bottom	0.0	0.0	1.9	1.7	2.3	2.1
2	0.0	0.0	2.7	2.6	3.3	3.3
3	0.3	1.1	3.9	3.9	4.6	4.5
4	2.8	3.8	5.1	5.3	6.0	6.0
5	6.0	6.6	6.8	7.3	7.5	7.7
6	9.0	9.5	8.8	9.1	9.1	9.5
7	12.1	12.0	11.0	11.1	11.1	11.2
8	15.4	15.1	13.7	13.6	13.5	13.4
9	20.4	19.2	17.5	17.2	16.5	16.5
Top	34.0	32.8	28.7	28.3	26.4	25.8
All	100.0	100.0	100.0	100.0	100.0	100.0
	Inequality Measure					
Gini	0.565	0.536	0.422	0.417	0.377	0.373
Theil	0.587	0.529	0.295	0.291	0.237	0.236

3.3 Adjusting for Household Size and Composition

We now proceed to the analysis of the distribution of income after adjustment for the size and composition of the household. As made clear in Chapter 2, no consensus exists on the most appropriate equivalence scale to make this adjustment, so we will be using the range of scales described there and assessing whether the choice of scale makes a significant difference to the results. We begin with the scale giving the value 1 to a single adult, 0.66 to each additional adult and 0.33 to each child (under 15). Figure 3.1 shows the distribution of disposable income, equivalised using this scale, among households in the 1994 and 1997 LII surveys.

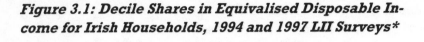

Figure 3.1: Decile Shares in Equivalised Disposable Income for Irish Households, 1994 and 1997 LII Surveys*

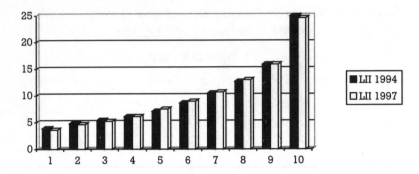

* See Table A2.1 in Appendix 2 for data.

A comparison with Table 3.1 shows that equivalisation produces a more equal distribution in each year. The share of the top decile is lower than before equivalisation, and the shares of the bottom two deciles are higher by what is, in proportion to their unadjusted share, a very substantial amount.

This reflects the fact that larger households have, on average, higher incomes than smaller households. Many of the households towards the bottom of the unadjusted distribution, for example, comprise single (often elderly) adults or couples. Comparing 1994 and 1997 we observe a similar pattern to that shown in Table 3.1 for unadjusted income. The bottom and top of the distribution lose share and deciles 5, 6, 7 and 8 all gain, the net result being little change in overall inequality as reflected in the summary measures.

Given the extent of uncertainty about the most appropriate way to adjust income for such differences, we need to test how sensitive these results are to alternative equivalence scales. The other four sets of equivalence scales described in Chapter 2 are now employed, to see whether the shape of the disposable income distribution is affected by the choice of scale. Table 3.3 shows decile shares among households in both the 1994 and 1997 LII surveys with each of these scales. We see the equalising impact of equivalisation occurs with each of the scales, and the shape of the distribution is very similar across all five sets of scales. Comparing 1994 and 1997, all the scales show once again the marked decline in share for the bottom of the distribution and the top decile which we saw in Table 3.3. While there are some differences across the scales in the exact pattern of change from 1994 to 1997, all show a substantial decline in share for the bottom half of the distribution and increase for the top half.

Up to this point, we have been concerned with the distribution of income among households. As discussed in Chapter 2, it makes sense to treat each household as a single unit and "count households" if no adjustment is made to income for differences in household size. When equivalent income is used, however, focusing on persons seems more appropriate since we are primarily concerned with the distribution of welfare or living standards among persons rather than households. Much of the previous research on the Irish income distribution refers to the distribution among households, and it is only on this basis that results from the 1973 and 1980 Household Budget Surveys are available. However, it is of interest to now also look at the distribution among persons, which is achieved by weighting each household in the analysis by the number of persons it contains. It must be emphasised that, as discussed in Chapter 2, the assumption is still being made that resources are distributed within the household so that each member of a given household has the same living standard: we are now in effect simply counting persons rather than households.

Table 3.3: Decile Shares in Equivalised Disposable Income for Irish Households in the 1994 and 1997 LII Surveys, Alternative Equivalence Scales

Decile	Share in Total Equivalised Disposable Income (%)							
	1/0.6/0.4 Scale		1/0.7/0.5 Scale		1/0.5/0.3 Scale		Square Root Scale	
	1994	*1997*	*1994*	*1997*	*1994*	*1997*	*1994*	*1997*
Bottom	3.8	3.5	3.6	3.4	3.9	3.5	3.6	3.3
2	4.7	4.5	4.8	4.7	4.6	4.4	4.4	4.1
3	5.4	5.2	5.5	5.2	5.3	5.2	5.1	5.0
4	6.1	6.2	6.1	6.2	6.1	6.1	6.1	6.4
5	7.1	7.4	7.1	7.3	7.2	7.6	7.4	7.7
6	8.7	9.0	8.5	8.8	8.9	9.1	9.0	9.2
7	10.5	10.6	10.4	10.6	10.7	10.9	10.9	11.2
8	12.8	13.1	12.5	12.8	12.9	13.1	12.9	13.1
9	15.9	15.9	16.0	16.2	15.8	15.7	16.0	15.8
Top	25.1	24.7	25.4	24.9	24.8	24.5	24.6	24.3
All	100.0	100.0	100.0	100.0	100.0	100.0	100.0	100.0

Table 3.4 compares the distributions of equivalised income (with the 1/0.66/0.33 scale) among households and among persons in the 1994 and 1997 LII surveys. We see that counting persons rather than households reduces the share of the top 30 per cent and increases the share of middle income groups in each year. Comparing the distribution among persons in 1997 with 1994 we do again see a shift in share away from the bottom 30 per cent, but this is less pronounced, and there is now little change at the top.

We go on in subsequent chapters to look at the evolution of the equivalised income distribution between 1987 and 1994, and to compare the shape of the equivalised distribution in Ireland and other countries. In the rest of this chapter, however, we explore some of the factors underlying the shape of the distribution in Ireland in 1994 and 1997, and why it has changed so markedly over that short period.

Table 3.4: Decile Shares in Equivalised Disposable Income Among Households and Among Persons, 1994 and 1997 LII Surveys (1/0.66/0.33 Scale)

| Decile | Share in Total Equivalised (1/0.66/0.33) Disposable Income (%) | | | |
| | *1994 LII* | | *1997 LII* | |
	Among Households	*Among Persons*	*Among Households*	*Among Persons*
Bottom	3.9	3.8	3.6	3.6
2	4.8	4.9	4.6	4.7
3	5.4	5.6	5.2	5.5
4	6.1	6.4	6.1	6.6
5	7.1	7.5	7.5	7.5
6	8.7	8.9	9.0	9.2
7	10.5	10.6	10.7	10.6
8	12.7	12.6	13.0	12.6
9	15.9	15.3	15.9	15.4
Top	25.0	24.4	24.6	24.3
All	100.0	100.0	100.0	100.0

3.4 SUB-GROUP DECOMPOSITION OF INEQUALITY IN 1994 AND 1997

We now employ a decomposition technique that allows us to assess the role of inequality between and within particular population sub-groups in overall inequality, and how this changed between 1994 and 1997. (Decomposition of inequality by sub-groups in this manner is discussed in, for example, Shorrocks (1980) and (1984) and Cowell (1995)). This is based on a summary inequality measure particularly suited for this purpose, called the mean logarithmic deviation (MLD). With this measure, overall inequality in the distribution can be conveniently decomposed into inequality between discrete sub-groups and inequality within each of those sub-groups. (The Gini coefficient, by contrast, cannot be readily decomposed in this way). Here we look at a range of household characteristics in this light, categorising households by age, by sex and then by labour force status of head, by composition type, and finally by the extent of social welfare recipiency.

We begin in Table 3.5 with three groups of households distinguished by whether the head is aged under 35, 35-64, or 65 or over. The table first shows the MLD for each of these sub-groups.

Table 3.5: Decomposition of Inequality in Disposable Equivalised Income by Age of Head, 1994 and 1997 LII Survey

Group	Inequality within Group (MLD*1000)	Group Mean Income (£ per week)	Group Share in Population (%)
A: 1994			
Under 35	162	132.13	18
35 – under 65	168	124.90	68
65 or over	102	107.20	14
All	160	123.64	100
Of which :			
Within group inequality (% of total)	158 (98.8)		
Between group inequality (% of total)	2 (1.2)		
B: 1997			
Under 35	175	177.65	19
35 – under 65	169	160.26	66
65 or over	121	132.17	15
All	167	159.35	100
Of which :			
Within group inequality (% of total)	163 (97.8)		
Between group inequality (% of total)	4 (2.2)		

We see that in both years the level of within-group inequality is much lower among those headed by someone aged 65 or over than among the two younger groups. Households headed by an older person also have lower mean income than the other two groups, even after adjustment for their smaller size. Inequality between the groups accounts for less than 2 per cent of overall inequality, the rest being attributable to inequality within the age groups. Inequality within each of the age-groups and between them all rose between 1994 and 1997.

Table 3.6 focuses on households headed by a man or a couple versus those with a female head.[2] Only 15 per cent of

---

[2] Nolan and Watson (1998) discuss alternatives to this crude categorisation.

households are in the latter group, and the table shows that the level of inequality is less than among them than the rest of the sample, but that female-headed households have lower mean incomes than the rest of the population. Inequality within these two groups rather than between them accounts for almost all the overall total, and this was unchanged between 1994 and 1997.

Table 3.6: Decomposition of Inequality in Disposable Equivalised Income by Sex of Head, 1994 and 1997 LII Survey

Group	Inequality within Group (MLD*1000)	Group Mean Income (£ per week)	Group Share in Population (%)
A: 1994			
Male or Couple	161	127.39	85
Female	134	103.14	15
All	160	123.64	100
Of which :			
Within group inequality (% of total)	157 (98.3)		
Between group inequality (% of total)	3 (1.7)		
B: 1997			
Male or Couple	164	164.61	86
Female	158	126.83	14
All	167	159.35	100
Of which :			
Within group inequality (% of total)	163 (97.7)		
Between group inequality (% of total)	4 (2.3)		

Table 3.7 categorises households by the labour force status of the head. There is now a great deal of variation in inequality within these groups. There is a much higher degree of inequality among households headed by a self-employed person (including farmers) than among those headed by an employee, and relatively little inequality among households headed by someone who is unemployed or ill, or engaged full-time in working in the home. There are also now substantial differences across the groups in mean equivalised income: households headed by an employee or a self-employed person have much higher mean incomes than those with an unemployed or

ill head or one working full-time in the home. In 1994, these differences in mean income across the groups accounted for about 27 per cent of the inequality in the overall sample. By 1997, the inequality produced by these differences in mean income had fallen, and accounted for 24 per cent of overall inequality. In terms of within-group inequality, there was a sharp increase for households headed by someone unemployed or ill. The size of some of the groups had also changed, with the proportion of employees increasing and unemployed falling.

Table 3.7: Decomposition of Inequality in Disposable Equivalised Income by Labour Force Status of Head, 1994 and 1997 LII Survey

Group	Inequality within Group (MLD*1000)	Group Mean Income (£ per week)	Group Share in Population (%)
A: 1994			
Employee	101	152.50	41
Self-employed	240	140.32	19
Unemployed/ill	55	69.59	17
Retired	105	112.34	12
Home Duties	75	82.92	10
All	160	123.64	100
Of which :			
Within group inequality (% of total)	116 (72.9)		
Between group inequality (% of total)	44 (27.1)		
B: 1997			
Employee	99	188.65	46
Self-employed	235	187.33	19
Unemployed/ill	100	86.16	14
Retired	116	142.96	13
Home Duties	65	93.73	9
All	167	159.35	100
Of which :			
Within group inequality (% of total)	128 (76.4)		
Between group inequality (% of total)	39 (23.6)		

Finally, it is interesting to focus on the role of social welfare transfers by distinguishing two groups: households which receive more than half their total income from transfers and households which do not. Table 3.8 shows that, unsurprisingly, the 30 per cent of households who do receive more than half their income from transfers have both lower mean equivalised income and lower within-group inequality than the rest of the sample. The table also shows that inequality between these two groups accounted for about 35 per cent of overall inequality in the 1994 sample.

Table 3.8: Decomposition of Inequality in Disposable Equivalised Income by Social Welfare Dependency, 1994 and 1997 LII Surveys

Group	Inequality within Group (MLD*1000)	Group Mean Income (£ per week)	Group Share in Population (%)
A: 1994			
Social Welfare 50% or Less of Total Income	136	147.33	70
Social Welfare More that 50% of Total Income	29	68.02	30
All	160	123.64	100
Of which :			
Within group inequality (% of total)	104 (65.2)		
Between group inequality (% of total)	56 (34.8)		
B: 1997			
Social Welfare 50% or Less of Total Income	137	183.83	76
Social Welfare More that 50% of Total Income	36	79.75	24
All	167	159.35	100
Of which :			
Within group inequality (% of total)	113 (67.9)		
Between group inequality (% of total)	54 (32.1)		

By 1997, inequality within both groups had increased, and accounted for a slightly larger share in total inequality than in 1994. This reflects the fact that although the mean income of those relying on social welfare lagged behind the overall mean between 1994 and 1997, the size of that group declined significantly from 30 per cent to 24 per cent of the sample, reducing the between-group component of inequality.

These decomposition results clearly provide valuable insights into the structure of income inequality in Ireland and how it has been changing. This is approached from another perspective in the next section, where we look at where different types of household tend to be located in the income distribution and how that has been evolving.

3.5 WHO IS WHERE IN THE INCOME DISTRIBUTION?

We begin by looking at the location of persons in the income distribution categorised by the age of the head of the household in which they live, and focus on the proportion falling into each quintile of the disposable equivalised income distribution among persons. (We employ quintiles — successive one-fifths of the distribution — rather than deciles in order to see the overall pattern more easily.) We see first in Figure 3.2 that people in households headed by someone aged between 35 and 64 were spread rather evenly over the quintiles in both 1994 and 1997. In 1994 those in households headed by someone aged under 35 were relatively heavily concentrated in both the bottom and the top quintile, but by 1997 they were more concentrated at the top. In 1994 those in households headed by someone aged 65 or over were heavily concentrated in the second quintile from the bottom. By 1997, however, the proportion at the top of the distribution had fallen and the numbers in the bottom quintile had risen markedly. The short period between 1994 and 1997 thus saw a considerable change at both the top and bottom of the distribution, to the advantage of younger households and the disadvantage of older ones.

Figure 3.2: Position in the Income Distribution of Persons Categorised by Age of Household Head, 1994 and 1997 LII Surveys*

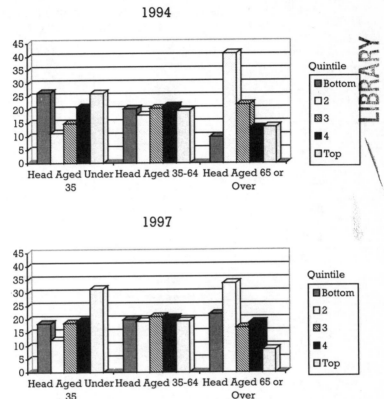

1994

1997

* See Table A2.2 in Appendix 2 for data.

Table 3.9 distinguishes those living in households headed by a couple or a single man and those headed by a woman. We see that the latter are significantly more heavily concentrated towards the bottom of the income distribution, and that their proportion in the bottom quintile increased from one-quarter to over one-third between 1994 and 1997.

Table 3.9: Position in the Income Distribution of Persons Categorised by Sex of Household Head, 1994 and 1997 LII Surveys

	Position in Equivalised (1/0.66/0.33) Disposable Income Distribution (%)	
Quintile	Male or Couple Head	Female Head
A: 1994		
Bottom	19.1	24.3
2	17.3	35.6
3	20.9	14.9
4	21.5	11.8
Top	21.2	13.4
All	100.0	100.0
B: 1997		
Bottom	17.4	35.7
2	19.2	24.9
3	20.6	15.8
4	21.2	13.0
Top	21.5	10.7
All	100.0	100.0

Figure 3.3 categorises people by the labour force status of the head of their household, and we see that those in households headed by an employee are mostly located in the top three quintiles. Those in households with a self-employed head are relatively heavily concentrated both at the bottom and at the top of the income distribution. Those in households headed by a farmer are fairly evenly spread over the distribution. Over 60 per cent of those in households headed by an unemployed person were in the bottom quintile in 1994, and by 1997 this had risen to 68 per cent. Those in households headed by a retired person were heavily concentrated in the second and third quintile from the bottom in 1994, but by 1997 the proportion in the bottom quintile had risen a good deal. Those in households where the head works full-time in the home were mostly in the bottom 2 quintiles in each year.

Figure 3.3: Position in the Income Distribution of Persons Categorised by Labour Force Status of Household Head, 1994 LII Survey*

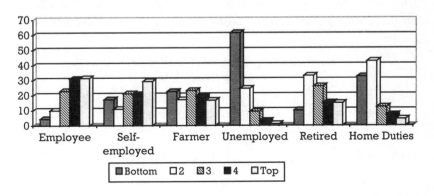

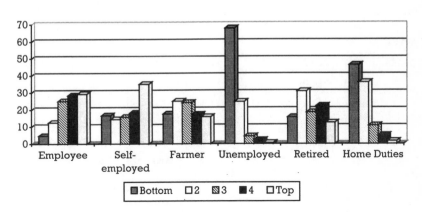

* See Table A2.3 in Appendix 2 for data.

Finally, Table 3.10 focuses on a categorisation by the number of adults and children in the household. This shows that those in 1-adult households were heavily concentrated in the second quintile from the bottom in 1994, and in the bottom quintile in 1997. Those in households comprising 1 adult with children were very heavily concentrated right at the bottom of the distribution, though less so in 1997 than in 1994. A relatively high proportion of those in households comprising couples with 1 or

2 children were towards the top of the distribution in both years. Those with 4 or more children, on the other hand, were very heavily concentrated in the bottom quintile.

Table 3.10: Position in the Income Distribution of Persons Categorised by Household Composition Type, 1994 LII Survey

	Position in Equivalised (1/0.66/0.33) Disposable Income Distribution (%)						
Quintile	*1 adult*	*2 adults*	*1 adult + children*	*2 adults, 1 child*	*2 adults, 2 children*	*2 adults, 3 children*	*2 adults, 4+ children*
A: 1994							
Bottom	21.2	9.2	56.4	14.0	12.4	22.5	37.0
2	35.3	26.9	17.8	15.7	8.8	15.5	14.2
3	9.5	16.2	18.1	12.4	20.5	16.6	22.9
4	10.0	16.8	6.2	23.6	28.6	27.2	19.0
Top	24.0	31.0	1.5	34.4	29.6	18.1	6.9
All	100.0	100.0	100.0	100.0	100.0	100.0	100.0
B: 1997							
Bottom	36.7	13.6	42.2	17.0	12.8	25.0	41.6
2	21.1	24.0	9.8	11.2	7.1	12.5	19.4
3	8.5	11.4	38.3	17.9	24.1	14.4	26.3
4	11.1	14.9	8.7	22.7	32.5	29.3	6.2
Top	22.7	36.0	1.0	31.3	23.6	18.8	6.6
All	100.0	100.0	100.0	100.0	100.0	100.0	100.0

3.6 INITIAL RESULTS FOR 1998

While we have been able to analyse the distribution of income in the 1997 Living in Ireland survey in some depth, data from the 1998 round of the survey is just now coming on stream. In concluding this chapter it is therefore valuable to look briefly at some initial results on the overall shape of the distribution in that sample. Once again it is important to be conscious of the fact that some attrition in the sample takes place from year to year, and that reweighting is employed to seek to maintain the overall representativeness of the results. A full description of the 1998 sample and a discussion of attrition and reweighting in that context is given in Layte *et al* (2000).

We look first in Table 3.11 at the distribution of disposable income among households, without adjustment for differences in household size and composition, in 1998 compared with 1997 and 1994. We see once again a decline in the share of the bottom 30 per cent of the distribution between 1997 and 1998, which is in fact more pronounced than that observed from 1994 to 1997. With the share of the top decile rising from 1997 to 1998, unlike 1994-97, the summary inequality measures also rise marginally.

Table 3.11: Decile Shares and Summary Inequality Measures, Disposable Income among Irish Households, 1994, 1997 and 1998 Living in Ireland Surveys

Households	Share in Total Disposable Income (%)		
Decile	*1994 LII*	*1997 LII*	*1998 LII*
Bottom	2.3	2.1	1.8
2	3.3	3.3	3.0
3	4.6	4.5	4.4
4	6.0	6.0	6.0
5	7.5	7.7	7.7
6	9.1	9.5	9.5
7	11.1	11.2	11.3
8	13.5	13.4	13.5
9	16.5	16.5	16.7
Top	26.4	25.8	26.1
All	100.0	100.0	100.0
	Inequality Measure		
Gini	0.377	0.373	0.386
Theil	0.237	0.236	0.251

Table 3.12 shows the distribution of market and gross income in the three years. Once again, the distribution among households of income from the market is seen to become if anything more equally-distributed from 1997 to 1998, as it did from 1994 to

1997. Turning to the distribution of gross income, there is once again some decline in share for the bottom 30 per cent from 1997 to 1998, as there had been from 1994 to 1997.

Table 3.12: Decile Shares for Direct and Gross Income among Households, 1994, 1997 and 1998 LII Survey

Decile	Share in Total Income (%)					
	Direct			*Gross*		
	1994	*1997*	*1998*	*1994*	*1997*	*1998*
Bottom	0.0	0.0	0.0	1.9	1.7	1.6
2	0.0	0.0	0.0	2.7	2.6	2.5
3	0.3	1.1	1.5	3.9	3.9	3.7
4	2.8	3.8	4.2	5.1	5.3	5.2
5	6.0	6.6	7.0	6.8	7.3	7.5
6	9.0	9.5	9.5	8.8	9.1	9.2
7	12.1	12.0	12.0	11.0	11.1	11.3
8	15.4	15.1	15.2	13.7	13.6	13.7
9	20.4	19.2	19.3	17.5	17.2	17.6
Top	34.0	32.8	31.4	28.7	28.3	27.7
All	100.0	100.0	100.0	100.0	100.0	100.0
	Inequality Measure					
Gini	0.565	0.536	0.520	0.422	0.417	0.418
Theil	0.587	0.529	0.495	0.295	0.291	0.291

Finally, Table 3.13 shows the distribution of income among households after adjusting for differences in size and composition using the 1/0.66/0.33 equivalence scale. We now see the share of the bottom 30 per cent of households down by 0.7 per cent of total income between 1997 and 1998. This brings the cumulative fall in the share of the bottom 30 per cent up to 1.4 per cent of total income over the 1994-98 period. A declining share for the top decile from 1994 to 1997 had offset this decline in terms of overall inequality as reflected in the summary measures. From 1997 to 1998, however, the share of the top decile rose and so did the summary inequality measures.

Table 3.13: Decile Shares in Equivalised Disposable Income for Irish Households, 1994,1997 and 1998 LII Surveys (1/0.66/0.33 Scale)

	Share in Total Equivalised (1/0.66/0.33) Disposable Income (%)		
Decile	*1994 LII*	*1997 LII*	*1998 LII*
Bottom	3.9	3.6	3.4
2	4.8	4.6	4.3
3	5.4	5.2	5.0
4	6.1	6.1	6.2
5	7.1	7.5	7.6
6	8.7	9.0	9.1
7	10.5	10.7	10.6
8	12.7	13.0	12.8
9	15.9	15.9	15.8
Top	25.0	24.6	25.2
All	100.0	100.0	100.0
	Inequality Measure		
Gini	0.326	0.329	0.338
Theil	0.184	0.185	0.195

3.7 CONCLUSIONS

This chapter has looked at the distribution of income among Irish households and persons in the 1990s, using data from household surveys carried out by the ESRI in 1994 and 1997 and some initial results from 1998.

Focusing on the period from 1994 to 1997, summary measures suggested little change in the overall level of inequality in the distribution of disposable income among Irish households over this period. There was however a shift away from the bottom 30 per cent and the top decile to the middle of the distribution. The distribution of income directly from the market was if anything more equally distributed among households in 1997 than 1994, but the equalising effects of social welfare transfers declined.

The shape of the disposable income distribution after adjustment for differences in household size and composition, using alternative equivalence scales, was seen to have changed in a similar way to the unadjusted distribution between 1994 and 1997. Focusing on the distribution among persons rather than households showed a decline in shares for the bottom but now little change at the top.

A decomposition analysis of the distribution of equivalised income in 1994 and 1997 looked at inequality within and between different groups of households, distinguished on the basis of age, gender, labour force status and social welfare dependence. For example, this showed that inequality between households categorised by the labour force status of the head accounted for about 27 per cent of overall inequality in 1994 and 24 per cent in 1997. Within these groups, inequality was highest for households headed by a self-employed person and lowest among the retired.

There were also some changes in the location of different types of household in the income distribution. Those in households headed by someone aged between 35 and 64 were spread rather evenly over the quintiles in both 1994 and 1997, but there were considerable shifts for both older and younger households. In particular, households headed by someone aged 65 or over were more heavily concentrated towards the bottom by 1997.

Initial results from the 1998 Living in Ireland survey showed a continued decline in the share of equivalised income going to the bottom 30 per cent of households. This brought the cumulative fall in the share of the bottom 30 per cent from 1994 to 1998 up to 1.4 per cent of total income. A declining share for the top decile from 1994 to 1997 had offset this decline in terms of overall inequality, but from 1997 to 1998 the share of that decile rose and so did summary inequality measures.

In assessing both the overall shape of the distribution of income in Ireland and these recent trends, a frame of reference is provided by comparison with corresponding figures for other countries. That is the topic of Chapter 5, but first we look in Chapter 4 at how the Irish distribution has been evolving over a longer period, back to the early 1970s.

Chapter 4

Trends in the Irish Income Distribution Since 1973

Brian Nolan

4.1 INTRODUCTION

So far we have focused on data from the household surveys carried out by the ESRI in the 1990s. In this chapter we use data from a household survey carried out by the ESRI in 1987, and from the Household Budget Surveys carried out by the CSO in 1973, 1980, 1987 and 1994/95, to see how the Irish income distribution has been evolving over a longer period. Section 4.2 looks at 1987 and 1994, for which estimates of the income distribution are available from both ESRI and HBS surveys. Section 4.3 documents trends in the distribution over the period from 1973 to 1997. Section 4.4 analyses factors underpinning these longer-term trends, while Section 4.5 presents an in-depth decomposition analysis of the 1987-1994 changes. Section 4.6 summarises the main findings.

4.2 THE INCOME DISTRIBUTION IN 1987 AND 1994

We look first at the distribution of disposable income among households in the ESRI and CSO samples for 1987 and 1994, in Table 4.1. (We concentrate now on the distribution among households rather than persons, because it is only on that basis that we can push the comparisons back to 1973 in the next section.) We see that in each of the years there was some difference between the estimates derived from the ESRI surveys and those from HBS, with the share going to the top decile rather higher in the ESRI surveys. However, both sets of surveys show a similar pattern of broad stability in the distribution between the two years.[1]

Table 4.1: Decile Shares in Disposable Income for Irish Households in 1987 and 1994, ESRI and HBS Surveys

	Share in Total Disposable Income (%)			
	1987		*1994*	
Decile	*ESRI*	*HBS*	*ESRI*	*HBS*
Bottom	2.0	2.2	2.3	2.1
2	3.4	3.7	3.3	3.5
3	4.8	5.0	4.6	4.8
4	5.9	6.3	6.0	6.0
5	7.3	7.6	7.5	7.6
6	8.8	9.2	9.1	9.2
7	10.7	11.0	11.1	11.3
8	13.2	13.4	13.5	13.6
9	16.5	16.5	16.5	16.7
Top	27.4	25.1	26.4	25.1
All	100.0	100.0	100.0	100.0

Turning to gross income, Table 4.2 shows the decile shares for the two years from the two sets of surveys. These again show a higher share going to the top decile in the ESRI surveys but only modest changes in shares between the two years.

---

[1] This stability is reflected in the Gini and Theil coefficients for the ESRI surveys, but comparable summary measures cannot be accurately computed from the HBS microdata because what is termed "top-coding" was employed in releasing these data to researchers. This involves setting very high incomes to a ceiling figure, which would distort the inequality measures. Decile shares however can be corrected for top-coding and this has been done for the figures presented here. Since mean income for the total sample without top-coding is published, total income can be calculated, the income of deciles 1-9 can be derived from the micro-data, and that for the top decile — affected by the top-coding — can be derived as a residual.

Table 4.2: Decile Shares in Gross Income for Irish Households in 1987 and 1994, ESRI and HBS Surveys

	Share in Total Gross Income (%)			
	1987		*1994*	
Decile	*ESRI*	*HBS*	*ESRI*	*HBS*
Bottom	1.7	1.9	1.9	1.9
2	2.8	3.1	2.7	2.9
3	4.0	4.2	3.9	4.0
4	5.2	5.4	5.1	5.3
5	6.7	7.0	6.8	6.9
6	8.6	8.8	8.8	8.9
7	10.7	11.0	11.0	11.2
8	13.5	13.6	13.7	13.8
9	17.6	17.6	17.5	17.5
Top	29.2	27.5	28.7	27.8
All	100.0	100.0	100.0	100.0

One important difference between the ESRI and HBS surveys is in the timing of the fieldwork, as mentioned in Chapter 2, and this may have had an impact on farm incomes in particular. However, the reasons for the divergence in the shape of the distribution are not clear at this point. As far as trends over the 1987-94 period are concerned, though, both sets of surveys support the same conclusion of little change in the distribution of gross and disposable income.

We now proceed to adjust for the size and composition of the household, beginning again with the 1/0.66/0.33 equivalence scale. Table 4.3 shows the distribution of gross and disposable income equivalised using this scale in the 1987 and 1994 ESRI surveys: analysis of equivalised incomes in the 1987 and 1994-95 HBS indicate very similar patterns over time.

Table 4.3: Decile Shares in Equivalised Gross and Disposable Income for Irish Households, 1987 and 1994 ESRI Surveys (1/0.66/0.33 Scale)

| | Share in Total Equivalised (1/0.66/0.33) Income (%) | | | |
| | *Gross* | | *Disposable* | |
Decile	*1987*	*1994*	*1987*	*1994*
Bottom	2.7	3.2	3.2	3.9
2	4.1	4.0	4.8	4.8
3	4.9	4.5	5.8	5.4
4	5.6	5.2	6.5	6.1
5	6.8	6.4	7.4	7.1
6	8.3	8.2	8.7	8.7
7	10.1	10.3	10.2	10.5
8	12.4	13.0	12.3	12.7
9	16.3	17.2	15.2	15.9
Top	28.8	28.1	25.9	25.0
All	100.0	100.0	100.0	100.0

We see that for gross income there is now some increase in the share of the bottom decile, with a decline in share for those in the middle of the distribution — deciles 3, 4, 5 and 6 — and for the top decile. For disposable income the increase in the share of the bottom decile is greater, at about two-thirds of one per cent of total income, while deciles 3, 4 and 5 and the top decile see a fall.

The other four sets of equivalence scales described in earlier chapters are now employed, to see whether the pattern of change between 1987 and 1994 is affected by the choice of scale. Table 4.4 shows decile shares in disposable income for both 1987 and 1994 with each of these scales. All show a marked increase in share for the bottom decile, and a fall in share for deciles 3, 4, 5 and the top decile.

Table 4.4: Decile Shares in Equivalised Disposable Income for Irish Households, 1987 and 1994 ESRI Surveys, Alternative Equivalence Scales

	Share in Total Equivalised Disposable Income (%)							
	Equivalence Scale							
	1/0.6/0.4		1/0.7/0.5		1/0.5/0.3		Square Root	
Decile	1987	1994	1987	1994	1987	1994	1987	1994
Bottom	3.1	3.8	3.0	3.6	3.2	3.9	3.1	3.6
2	4.8	4.7	4.7	4.8	4.8	4.6	4.5	4.4
3	5.7	5.4	5.8	5.5	5.6	5.3	5.3	5.1
4	6.5	6.1	6.6	6.1	6.4	6.1	6.3	6.1
5	7.4	7.1	7.4	7.1	7.4	7.2	7.4	7.4
6	8.6	8.7	8.6	8.5	8.7	8.9	8.8	9.0
7	10.2	10.5	10.0	10.4	10.3	10.7	10.4	10.9
8	12.3	12.8	12.2	12.5	12.4	12.9	12.6	12.9
9	15.3	15.9	15.3	16.0	15.3	15.8	15.6	16.0
Top	26.1	25.1	26.4	25.4	25.9	24.8	26.0	24.6
All	100.0	100.0	100.0	100.0	100.0	100.0	100.0	100.0

The increase between 1987 and 1994 in the share of total income going to the very bottom of the income distribution is consistent with the pattern of declining income poverty gaps over the period reported in Callan *et al.* (1996). An important factor at work there was the extent to which the lowest social welfare payments were brought up relatively rapidly, as the recommendations of the Commission on Social Welfare in this regard were implemented. This meant that Unemployment Assistance, for example, rose a good deal more rapidly than both social welfare pensions and average earnings (see Callan *et al.*, 1996 for a discussion). We now move on to overall trends in the distribution over the longer period back to 1973.

4.3 THE IRISH INCOME DISTRIBUTION FROM THE EARLY 1970s TO THE MID-1990s

We now look at the distribution of income among households over the longer period back to the early 1970s, using the HBS samples for each of the years for which these are available. The HBS was carried out in 1973 and 1980, and although the micro-data from these surveys are not available for analysis some figures have been produced by the CSO, published in Murphy (1984, 1985) and Rottman and Reidy (1988). Table 4.5 shows the decile shares in disposable income among households from the HBS for 1973, 1980, 1987 and 1994/95. It also shows Gini and Theil summary measures computed from these decile shares: while these will understate the extent of inequality at each point in time (because inequality within each decile is ignored) they should capture trends over time adequately.

Table 4.5: Decile Shares in Disposable Income among Irish Households, 1973, 1980, 1987 and 1994/95 HBS

Decile	Share in Total Disposable Income (%)			
	1973	1980	1987	1994-95
Bottom	1.7	1.7	2.2	2.1
2	3.3	3.5	3.7	3.5
3	5.0	5.1	5.0	4.8
4	6.5	6.6	6.3	6.0
5	7.8	7.9	7.6	7.6
6	9.2	9.3	9.2	9.2
7	10.9	11.0	11.0	11.3
8	13.0	13.0	13.4	13.6
9	16.2	16.2	16.6	16.7
Top	26.4	25.7	25.0	25.1
All	100.0	100.0	100.0	100.0
Gini	0.367	0.360	0.352	0.362
Theil	0.221	0.211	0.200	0.210

Source: Decile shares for 1973 and 1980 from Rottman and Reidy (1988), Table 7.4, for 1987 and 1994/95 from microdata tapes (with correction for top-coding).

Looking first at 1973 to 1980, we see that the share of the bottom decile was unchanged but those of deciles 2-7 all rose slightly, with the top decile seeing a substantial decline in share. This is reflected in the fall in the Gini and Theil coefficients, also shown in the table. Between 1980 and 1987, the share of the bottom quintile rose substantially and that of the top decile again fell. Deciles 3-6 now experience a decline in share, however, with deciles 8 and 9 seeing an increase. The Gini and Theil coefficients show a further decline in inequality between 1980 and 1987. Over the whole period 1973-87, then, the HBS shows inequality in the distribution of disposable household income falling, and the Gini coefficient falling from 0.37 to 0.35. This reflects the fact that the share of the top decile was down by 1.4 per cent of total income and that of the bottom quintile up by 0.9 per cent. It is worth noting that the other gainers were not in the bottom half of the distribution, but rather deciles 8 and 9.[2]

This pattern contrasts with the increase in inequality observed for gross income, over both sub-periods and 1973-87 as a whole. The redistributive impact of income tax and employees' social insurance contributions on the gross income distribution therefore increased substantially over the period, as seen in the growing gap between the summary inequality measures for gross and disposable income. In 1973 the Gini coefficient for disposable income was 97 per cent of that for gross income, in 1980 it had fallen to 94 per cent, and by 1987 it was only 88 per cent, while the corresponding percentages for the Theil measure were 93 per cent in 1973, 87 per cent in 1980 and 77 per cent in 1987.[3]

We saw in the previous section that the decline in inequality in the distribution of disposable income between 1973 and 1987 was not sustained after 1987. It would be desirable to look at trends during the earlier period having adjusted household incomes for differences in size and composition, in other words to analyse the distribution of equivalent household incomes. Without micro-data for 1973 and 1980, however, we have to draw on published results for those years. Roche (1984) presented equivalent gross and disposable income distributions

---

[2] In terms of Lorenz curves, 1980 and 1987 both Lorenz-dominate 1973. The Lorenz curve for 1987 lies inside that for 1980 at most points, but those curves cross and there is no unambiguous dominance.

[3] Murphy (1984) and Rottman and Reidy (1988) note that between 1973 and 1980 inequality rose even more for market income — that is, income before cash transfers — but transfers offset some of this increase.

for 1973 and 1980 using a set of equivalence scales based on
the social security rates paid at the start of the period. On this
basis the distribution of gross equivalent income became less
equal between 1973 and 1980, with the shares of each of the
bottom five deciles falling. For disposable income the picture
was less clear-cut: the share of the bottom decile fell between
the two years, that of the bottom half was unchanged, the top
decile lost share, and the remainder of the top half gained,
while the Gini coefficient indicates a fall in inequality.

The overall trends between the 1980 and 1987 HBS with
equivalised income were broadly similar to those in unadjusted
income — that is, the gap between gross and disposable income
distributions widened, with the former becoming if anything less
equal and the latter if anything more equal. The ESRI survey for
1987 points in the same direction: comparing unadjusted and
equivalent income distributions in the ESRI survey does suggest
that the gap between the two was wider than in 1980.

It is important to place these trends in the shape of the income distribution in the context of the evolution of average real
incomes. This is particularly important in comparing the 1970s,
1980s and 1990s because the pattern of real income growth was
very different in the three sub-periods analysed here, that is
1973-1980, 1980-1987, and 1987-1994. Between 1973 and 1980,
real incomes grew rapidly. Mean household income in the HBS
in 1980 was 193 per cent higher than in 1973, while the Consumer Price Index rose by 155 per cent, representing a 25 per
cent rise in average income in real terms. Between 1980 and
1987, on the other hand, average incomes rose by 87 per cent
in nominal terms but the CPI was 91 per cent higher by the end
of the period, so real incomes actually fell. Between 1987 and
1994, real incomes increased very substantially: average
household income rose by about 40 per cent while consumer
prices rose by only 22 per cent. The period from 1994 to 1997
also saw real income growth accelerate, with average household income rising by 23 per cent compared with only 6 per
cent for consumer prices.[4]

---

[4] This pattern of real income growth underlies the relationships between
Generalised Lorenz curves — discussed in Chapter 2 — for the different

4.4 EXPLAINING TRENDS IN INEQUALITY 1973-1994

Why then did inequality in the Irish income distribution evolve in this way over the years 1973-1994? Without micro-data for the earlier years it is not possible to address this question directly for the whole period using the type of decomposition analysis presented in the previous chapter for 1994-97. We have carried out such analyses for the 1987-94 period and discuss the results below, but it is worthwhile to first point to some likely links over the entire period between the income distribution and developments in the macroeconomy and in tax and social security policy. The central features of the Irish economic landscape in the 1970s and 1980s from this point of view were the striking increases in both unemployment and direct personal taxation.

Rising unemployment is likely to have been a major influence on the gross income distribution. The rate of unemployment doubled to 7-8 per cent of the labour force between 1973 and 1980.[5] A detailed analysis of within-group and between-group inequality in the 1973 and 1980 HBS was carried out by Murphy (1984) from within the CSO. This suggested that the increasing number of households with an unemployed or retired head or with no earner was primarily responsible for the increasing inequality in market incomes, with little increase in within-group inequality.[6] The impact on the distribution of gross incomes was ameliorated though not fully offset by the fact that rates of social security support grew relatively rapidly. This was particularly marked for the elderly, which would have been an important influence on the share of the bottom quintile in the unadjusted distribution. The unemployed, on the other hand,

---

years. For disposable income without any adjustment for household size, generalised Lorenz curves for both 1980 and 1987 lie above 1973 at all points. The curves for 1980 and 1987 themselves cross — because mean income is slightly lower (in real terms) but the income share of the bottom deciles is slightly higher in 1987 than 1980 — so no unambiguous ranking in welfare terms is produced. However 1994 lies above 1987 at all points, and the same is true for 1997 versus 1994.

[5] The rate of unemployment in the Labour Force Survey carried out in April 1980 was 7.3 per cent, while registered unemployment over the year averaged over 8 per cent.

[6] See Murphy (1984) p. 84.

tend to be most heavily concentrated in the bottom half but not
the bottom quintile of the unadjusted distribution, which experienced declining shares in total gross income.

Between 1980 and 1987 unemployment increased very
much more rapidly, rising to over 18 per cent of the labour
force. This is likely to have played a major part in the falling
gross income shares of the second and third quintiles of the unadjusted distribution. In assessing the impact on household incomes, it is worth noting that in the Irish case an unusually high
proportion of the unemployed are married men living in families, who would conventionally be termed "household heads",
rather than secondary earners.[7] Despite the fact that once again
social security support rates were increased in real terms over
the period, unemployment did in general result in a decline in
income for those affected.[8] In the Irish case a particularly high
proportion of the unemployed have also been away from work
long-term: by 1987 about half of all men on the Live Register of
the unemployed had been in that position for more than one
year. A substantial majority of the unemployed have therefore
exhausted unemployment insurance entitlements and have to
rely on (what were in 1987 lower) means-tested social assistance payments.

Between 1973 and 1980, total tax revenue (including social
security contributions) rose from 31 per cent to 34 per cent of
GDP.[9] Within that increasing total, taxes on personal income
plus employees' social security contributions became more important, rising from 29 per cent of total taxation in 1973 to 37
per cent in 1980.[10] This sharp increase in taxation and particularly personal taxation reflected not only the growing burden of
unemployment on the public purse, but also the expansion in
other areas of state expenditure associated with the ill-fated fiscal policy adopted in 1977-1979. This was intended to be a
counter-cyclical employment-creating strategy, but its lasting

---

[7] See OECD Employment Outlook (1990); NESC (1990).

[8] For example, Callan and Nolan (1999) show that in most cases the replace-
ment rate is below 80 per cent in the 1994 LII sample.

[9] OECD Revenue Statistics (1990) Table 3.

[10] OECD Revenue Statistics (1990) Tables 11 and 15.

result was an extremely high level of public debt and associated debt service payments. After 1980, as the public sector deficit was brought under control, total tax revenue rose by even more, reaching 40 per cent of GDP in 1987. Taxes on personal income and employees' social security contributions continued to play a more and more important role, and by 1987 were accounting for 40 per cent of all tax revenue. (The increase in direct tax revenue was achieved not by raising top tax rates — the top rate was in fact considerably lower in 1987 than in the early 1970s — but by a higher standard rate and by failure to index allowances and tax bands to take inflation into account.) [11]

The growing redistributive impact of income tax and social security contributions over the 1973-87 period was attributable to both their growing importance and to the increasing degree of progressivity with which these taxes operated. Table 4.6 shows the average tax rate for income tax and for social insurance contributions in the HBS, and a summary measure of progressivity known as the Suits index. This measure is based on the share of total tax paid by different income groups versus their share in total income; it has a positive value for a progressive tax and is negative for a regressive one.

We see first that in 1973 income tax and employees' social security contributions came to just under 10 per cent of gross income of sample households. By 1980 this had risen to 15 per cent, as the general level of taxation rose and income taxation accounted for a steadily rising share of the total. Between 1980 and 1987 the percentage of gross income going in income tax again increased, though less dramatically, but now social security contributions rose substantially.

---

[11] In the early/mid-1970s Irish income tax rates started at about 25 per cent and rose as high as 80 per cent, whereas in 1987 they went from 35 per cent to 58 per cent.

Table 4.6: Suits Progressivity Index and Average Tax Rate for Income Tax and PRSI Contributions, 1973, 1980, 1987 and 1994/95

	1973	1980	1987	1994/95
Average Tax Rate (%)				
Income tax	7.8	12.9	15.4	14.2
PRSI contributions	2.0	2.2	3.5	3.7
Total	9.8	15.1	18.9	17.8
Suits Progressivity Index				
Income tax	0.194	0.207	0.275	0.282
PRSI contributions	-0.074	0.056	0.133	0.147
Total	0.138	0.185	0.249	0.254

Source: Figures for 1973 from Nolan (1981), for 1980, 1987 and 1994-95 calculated from HBS Reports.

Focusing on the degree of progressivity, Nolan (1981) used the Suits progressivity index to show that in 1973 income tax was progressive but social security contributions were mildly regressive (as indicated by the negative value of the index).[12] From Table 4.6 we see that by 1980 income tax was slightly more progressive but social insurance contributions were now also progressive.[13] Between 1980 and 1987, income tax became a good deal more progressive and so did social insurance contributions. However, contributions became a more important element in the total over this period and remained a good deal less progressive than income tax. The net result was that the Suits index for income tax plus social insurance contributions together rose by almost as much between 1973-1980 as between 1980-1987, registering an increase of 34 per cent in the earlier period and 35 per cent in the later one. Between 1987

---

[12] The index is calculated on the basis of share of tax paid by gross income groups and the share of gross income they receive.

[13] Murphy (1984) presents the Suits (and Kakwani) progressivity index calculated for equivalent (market) income for 1973 and 1980. Like Table 4.6 (based on unadjusted gross income), this showed the degree of progressivity of income tax little changed and that of employees' social security contributions significantly increased between 1973 and 1980.

and 1994, the Suits index rose marginally for both income tax and social insurance contributions, but they both now declined as a proportion of gross income.

We can analyse in more depth the way the income distribution evolved between 1987 and 1994, by exploiting the fact that microdata is available for those years. We do this by carrying out for 1987 the same sub-group decomposition analysis that we presented for 1994 and 1997 in Chapter 3, using the mean log deviation inequality measure. Decomposition by labour force status was the one to reveal the most substantial changes between 1994 and 1997, and this also turned out to be the case for 1987-1994 so we concentrate on those results here. Table 4.7 shows that in 1987 inequality between the groups accounted for 13 per cent of overall inequality, whereas by 1994 this had risen to 27 per cent. This reflects the fact that there was less variation in mean incomes across the groups in 1987, as well as the higher inequality within certain groups — notably the self-employed, the unemployed or ill, and households headed by someone working full-time in the home — in that year. Thus by 1994 inequality within these groups had declined while the differences between the groups in mean incomes had widened, with households headed by someone who was unemployed or ill, or working full-time in the home, falling further behind the average.

Table 4.7: Decomposition of Inequality in Disposable Equivalised Income by Labour Force Status of Head, 1987 ESRI Survey

Group	Inequality within group (MLD*1000)	Group mean Income (£ per week)	Group share in population (%)
A: 1987			
Employee	105	94.02	44
Self-employed	382	92.62	22
Unemployed/ill	97	50.60	19
Retired	114	77.68	9
Home duties	148	67.64	7
All	194	82.33	100
Of which :			
Within group inequality (% of total)	168 (86.6)		
Between group inequality (% of total)	26 (13.4)		
B: 1994			
Employee	101	152.50	41
Self-employed	240	140.32	19
Unemployed/ill	55	69.59	17
Retired	105	112.34	12
Home duties	75	82.92	10
All	160	123.64	100
Of which :			
Within group inequality (% of total)	116 (72.9)		
Between group inequality (% of total)	44 (27.1)		

4.6 CONCLUSIONS

This chapter has used data from household surveys to see how the Irish income distribution has changed over the period back to 1973 – which is as far back as these surveys allow one to go. For 1987 and 1994, information is available from surveys carried out by the ESRI and by the CSO. There was some difference between the income distribution estimates derived from these sources, with the share going to the top decile rather higher in the ESRI surveys. However, both sets of surveys show a similar pattern of broad stability in the distribution of disposable income among households between the two years. When equivalence scales are used to adjust disposable income for differences in household size and composition, the share of the bottom decile is seen to have risen significantly, at the expense of those in the middle of the distribution and the top decile.

Over the period 1973-87 inequality in the distribution of disposable household income fell markedly, with the share of the top decile down by 1.4 per cent of total income and that of the bottom quintile up by 0.9 per cent. The share of the top decile fell both from 1973 to 1980 and from 1980 to 1987, but the increase for the bottom decile was in the latter period. An important factor at work was the increasingly redistributive impact of income tax and employees' social insurance contributions, reflecting both increasing progressivity and a very substantial increase in the average tax rate. From 1987 to 1994 this continued but at a much slower rate, helping to explain the greater stability in the shape of the distribution over those years.

Chapter 5

Ireland's Income Distribution in International Perspective

Brian Nolan and Bertrand Maître

5.1 INTRODUCTION

We have looked at the shape of the income distribution in Ireland and how it has been changing, but a comparative perspective is also essential if we are to know what to make of these results. The aim of this chapter is thus to compare the distribution of income in Ireland with other countries. Great care is needed in making such comparisons: without careful attention to comparability in terms of income concept, income unit, time period, nature and coverage of data source, equivalence scale (where relevant) and so on, misleading conclusions can be reached. Much of the chapter is taken up with a comparison based on data for the mid-1990s from the European Community Household Panel (ECHP), which has the major advantage of being a harmonised survey across all the participating countries, covering most of the EU. We then look at available comparisons for the 1980s, relying mostly on the income distribution database assembled by the Luxembourg Income Study (LIS) which for Ireland includes data from the 1987 ESRI survey. We then draw on the results of some recent comparative analyses of income inequality carried out by the OECD, which once again for Ireland relies on data provided from the ESRI surveys.

The chapter is structured as follows. Section 5.2 looks at the distribution of income in Ireland versus other EU member countries in the first two waves of the European Community Household Panel survey. Section 5.3 compares these with results from other cross-country studies for earlier periods. Section 5.4 discusses the results of the OECD comparative study of inequality trends, and Section 5.5 brings together the chapter's conclusions.

5.2 THE DISTRIBUTION OF INCOME IN THE ECHP

A full description of the ECHP dataset in terms of sampling, response rates, weighting procedures etc. is in Eurostat (1999). Here we present some results we have derived from Wave 1, carried out in 1994, then look at any major changes by Wave 2, carried out in 1995.

The ECHP survey contains detailed information on income accruing to household members from different sources, such as income from employment, income from self-employment, occupational pensions, rental income, interest and dividends, cash transfers from the state by type, and regular cash transfers from other households. For some income sources, notably the main income from employment, information is sought on both gross receipt and on net receipt after deductions of tax and social insurance contributions. For a number of other sources, notably self-employment, rental and investment income, only gross or net receipts were obtained. The nature of the data obtained for certain countries raises particular problems in this respect. For France, for example, self-employment income is only available on a gross basis and no imputation of net income was included on the ECHP file. Some households in the dataset could not be included in our analysis because they had missing values for total household income — this was a particularly serious problem for Italy.

Unlike the data used in this study so far, the reference period covered by the income questions is annual for all sources, in the case of Wave 1 relating to the calendar year 1993 and for Wave 2 to 1994. The Irish element of the ECHP, the Living in Ireland Survey, collected information on both current and annual income. Table 5.1 shows the distribution of annual disposable income in Ireland in 1993 from wave 1 of the ECHP, compared with the estimates based on current income in 1994 from the same survey presented in Chapter 3 above. The bottom half of the income distribution looks very similar, but there are differences in the top half. The share of the top decile in annual income is a good deal higher than the share of that decile in the current income distribution, balanced by lower shares for the rest of the top half. The shorter accounting period would in itself lead one to expect the current distribution to be less equal than the annual one, though empirical studies with UK data suggest not markedly so (see Nolan, 1986). The reasons for this difference merit in-depth investigation, though this is complicated by the fact that the ECHP data are processed internally by Eurostat, including imputation of missing values.

Table 5.1: Decile Shares in Disposable Income among Irish Households, Current versus Annual Income, 1994 Living in Ireland Survey/ECHP

	Share in Total Disposable Income (%)	
Decile	*Current*	*Annual*
Bottom	2.3	2.2
2	3.3	3.2
3	4.6	4.5
4	6.0	5.8
5	7.5	7.3
6	9.1	8.8
7	11.1	10.7
8	13.5	13.0
9	16.5	16.2
Top	26.4	28.3
All	100.0	100.0

Table 5.2 shows decile shares in disposable income among households in each country in Wave 1 of the ECHP, without any adjustment for differences in household size and composition. (As noted earlier, it seems appropriate to employ household weights when dealing with unequivalised incomes.)

Table 5.2 : Decile Shares in Disposable Income among Households, Wave1 ECHP

Share in Unequivalised Income (%)

Decile	Germany	Denmark	Neth.	Belgium	Luxem.	France	UK	**Ireland**	Italy	Greece	Spain	Portugal
1	2.3	2.9	2.5	2.4	2.5	2.2	2.0	**2.2**	2.1	1.4	2.3	1.5
2	4.0	4.4	4.2	4.0	4.2	4.0	3.3	**3.2**	3.9	3.1	3.6	2.7
3	5.4	5.5	5.5	5.1	5.3	5.2	4.4	**4.5**	5.3	4.5	4.9	3.9
4	6.6	6.6	6.9	6.3	6.5	6.5	5.6	**5.8**	6.4	6.0	6.2	5.4
5	7.9	8.0	8.4	7.7	7.7	7.8	7.2	**7.3**	7.8	7.5	7.5	7.0
6	9.4	9.6	9.8	9.2	8.9	9.1	9.0	**8.8**	9.1	9.0	8.8	8.6
7	11.1	11.5	11.4	11.2	10.6	10.7	10.9	**10.7**	11.0	10.9	10.5	10.3
8	13.1	13.3	13.1	13.4	12.6	12.8	13.1	**13.0**	13.2	13.3	12.8	12.8
9	15.9	15.5	15.5	16.3	15.4	15.9	16.5	**16.2**	16.4	16.6	16.3	17.3
10	24.5	22.9	22.6	24.3	26.3	25.8	28.0	**28.3**	24.9	27.8	27.1	30.6
Total	100.0	100.0	100.0	100.0	100.0	100.0	100.0	**100.0**	100.0	100.0	100.0	100.0

We see that there is considerable variation across countries in the share of total disposable income going to for example the bottom and the top deciles. The share of the bottom decile ranges from well under 2 per cent in Greece and Portugal up to almost 3 per cent in Denmark. Ireland, at just over 2 per cent, is not unusual. The share going to the top decile, on the other hand, ranges from 23-24 per cent in Denmark, the Netherlands and Belgium, up to over 30 per cent in Portugal. Ireland, at 28 per cent, is towards the upper end of the spectrum in that case, similar to the UK and Greece.

Various summary inequality measures for the distribution of disposable income among households are presented in Table 5.3.

Table 5.3: Summary Inequality Measures for Distribution of Disposable Income among Households, Wave 1 ECHP, 1993

	Gini	Rank	Atk 0.5	Rank	Atk 1	Rank	Theil	Rank
Netherlands	0.318	1	0.085	2	0.177	2	0.170	1
Denmark	0.320	2	0.085	1	0.163	1	0.178	2
Germany	0.343	3	0.097	3	0.194	4	0.197	3
Belgium	0.348	4	0.099	4	0.200	5	0.201	4
Luxembourg	0.350	5	0.100	5	0.190	3	0.213	6
Italy	0.354	6	0.103	6	0.207	7	0.209	5
France	0.355	7	0.106	7	0.202	6	0.220	7
Spain	0.373	8	0.113	8	0.216	8	0.238	8
Ireland	**0.393**	**9**	**0.126**	**9**	**0.235**	**9**	**0.270**	**10**
UK	0.395	10	0.127	10	0.244	10	0.268	9
Greece	0.401	11	0.136	11	0.267	11	0.282	11
Portugal	0.434	12	0.155	12	0.295	12	0.324	12

Ranked by the Gini measure, we see that Denmark and the Netherlands have the most equal distribution and Portugal and Greece have the least equal. Of the rest, Germany, Belgium and Luxembourg are towards the relatively equally distributed end of the spectrum, France, Italy and Spain are in the middle, and Ireland is with the UK towards the relatively unequal end of the scale. The other summary inequality measures, the Theil index and the Atkinson measure with parameter 0.5 or 1.0, show a broadly similar picture to the Gini, though with some variation in the individual rankings. Since we have not yet adjusted income for household size these rankings cannot be taken as reflecting the distribution of command over resources, living standards or welfare, but they provide a point of departure in comparing income distributions across the countries.

We now adjust household incomes to take differences in size and composition into account. Following recent Eurostat practice in such comparisons we employ the modified OECD scale as our central scale — that is, the first adult in the household is given a value of 1, each additional adult a value of 0.5, and each child a value of 0.3. To assess the overall sensitivity of these results we also use the so-called OECD scale (1/0.7/0.5) and the square root of household size scale employed in a number of comparative income distribution studies. We focus on the distribution of equivalised income among persons, each individual being attributed the equivalised disposable income of their household.

Table 5.4 shows decile shares in equivalised disposable income among persons in the ECHP, using the modified OECD equivalence scale. As was the case for Ireland, equivalisation produces a more equal distribution, the share of the bottom decile is now higher in all countries than it was with unadjusted income, and the share going to the top decile is consistently lower. The former ranges from about 2 per cent in Greece and Portugal up to 4 ½ per cent in Denmark, while the latter ranges from 20 per cent in Denmark up to 29 per cent in Portugal. The bottom decile in Ireland now has a relatively high share, at over 3 per cent, but at 26 per cent the top decile also has a rather high share, similar to the UK.

Summary inequality measures for Wave 1 income equivalised using the modified OECD scale are shown in Table 5.5. The rankings in terms of the Gini measure are generally similar to those for unadjusted income, although Denmark rather than the Netherlands now has the most equal distribution and Portugal and Greece now have the least equal distributions, followed by the UK and then Ireland.

Table 5.4 : Decile Shares in Equivalised Disposable Income among Persons Wave 1 ECHP, 1993

Share in Equivalised Income (%)

Decile	Germany	Denmark	Neth.	Belgium	Lux.	France	UK	Ireland	Italy	Greece	Spain	Portugal
1	2.6	4.4	3.7	3.0	3.3	3.1	2.7	**3.3**	2.3	2.1	2.6	1.9
2	5.0	6.3	5.7	5.2	4.8	5.0	4.3	**4.5**	4.6	4.0	4.5	3.7
3	6.4	7.3	6.6	6.4	6.2	6.0	5.4	**5.3**	5.8	5.4	5.6	5.0
4	7.5	8.2	7.4	7.5	6.9	7.0	6.5	**6.2**	7.0	6.7	6.7	6.3
5	8.5	8.9	8.3	8.6	7.9	8.1	7.7	**7.4**	8.2	7.9	7.7	7.4
6	9.6	9.7	9.4	9.8	9.0	9.2	9.0	**8.7**	9.5	9.2	9.0	8.6
7	10.8	10.5	10.6	10.9	10.3	10.5	10.5	**10.4**	11.0	10.8	10.4	10.0
8	12.3	11.6	12.3	12.4	12.2	12.1	12.5	**12.4**	12.9	12.7	12.5	12.1
9	14.8	13.3	14.5	14.5	15.2	14.8	15.2	**15.5**	15.3	15.3	15.6	15.8
10	22.4	19.8	21.7	21.9	24.4	24.3	26.3	**26.4**	23.5	26.1	25.5	29.3
Total	100.0	100.0	100.0	100.0	100.0	100.0	100.0	**100.0**	100.0	100.0	100.0	100.0

Equivalence scale: modified OECD, 1, 0.5, 0.3.

Table 5.5: Summary Inequality Measures for Distribution of Equivalised (Modified OECD Scale) Disposable Income among Persons, Wave 1 ECHP, 1993

	Gini	Rank	Atk 0.5	Rank	Atk 1	Rank	Theil	Rank
Denmark	0.222	1	0.045	1	0.079	1	0.102	1
Netherlands	0.270	2	0.062	2	0.122	2	0.127	2
Belgium	0.282	3	0.068	3	0.132	3	0.139	3
Germany	0.293	4	0.073	4	0.146	4	0.149	4
France	0.309	5	0.081	6	0.154	6	0.174	6
Luxembourg	0.311	6	0.080	5	0.150	5	0.171	5
Italy	0.321	7	0.088	7	0.174	7	0.177	7
Spain	0.338	8	0.095	8	0.184	9	0.198	8
Ireland	**0.341**	**9**	**0.095**	**9**	**0.180**	**8**	**0.210**	**9**
UK	0.346	10	0.099	10	0.186	10	0.212	10
Greece	0.353	11	0.106	11	0.203	11	0.224	11
Portugal	0.388	12	0.125	12	0.238	12	0.264	12

To allow the sensitivity of the results to the choice of equivalence scale to be seen, we recalculated the decile shares and summary inequality measures for both the OECD and square root equivalence scales. Table 5.6 summarises the overall pattern by simply reporting the Gini inequality measure for each country with each of the three equivalence scales. We see that the equivalence scale employed does make a difference to the level of the Gini coefficient in some countries. However, while some pairwise rankings of countries by inequality level are different, the overall pattern in terms of country groupings is not affected by the choice across these three scales. In particular, from an Irish perspective it does not affect the placing of Ireland in a group with the UK, Greece and Spain, having the highest level of inequality other than Portugal.

Table 5.6: Gini Coefficient for Equivalised Disposable Income Among Persons in ECHP Wave 1, 1993, Alternative Equivalence Scales

	Gini Modified OECD Scale	Ranking	OECD Scale	Ranking	Square Root scale	Ranking
Denmark	0.22	1	0.23	1	0.23	1
Netherlands	0.27	2	0.28	2	0.27	2
Belgium	0.28	3	0.29	3	0.29	3
Germany	0.29	4	0.30	4	0.29	3
France	0.31	5	0.32	5	0.31	5
Luxembourg	0.31	5	0.32	5	0.31	5
Italy	0.32	7	0.33	7	0.32	7
Spain	0.34	8	0.34	8	0.34	8
Ireland	**0.34**	**8**	**0.35**	**9**	**0.34**	**8**
UK	0.35	10	0.35	9	0.35	10
Greece	0.35	10	0.36	11	0.35	10
Portugal	0.39	12	0.39	12	0.39	12

Income distribution results can also be derived from Wave 2 of the ECHP. Gini coefficients for Wave 2 (using the modified OECD scale) are compared with the estimates we derived from Wave 1 in Table 5.7. We see that the estimates for Wave 2 are generally similar to those for Wave 1, though the Wave 2 Gini is rather higher in Denmark and The Netherlands, and lower in France, the UK, Spain and Portugal.[1]

---

[1] Income distribution results based on Wave 2 of the ECHP have been published by Eurostat (Eurostat 1999). The Gini coefficients shown differ at most only marginally from the ones presented here except for Ireland, where 0.35 rather than 0.33 is given: this reflects on-going revisions to the data, our results being based on a later data release.

Table 5.7: Gini Coefficient for Equivalised Disposable Income among Persons in ECHP Wave 1, 1993, and Wave 2, 1994, Modified OECD Scale

	Gini			
	Wave 1 (1993)	*Ranking*	*Wave 2 (1994)*	*Ranking*
Denmark	0.22	1	0.24	1
Netherlands	0.27	2	0.29	4
Belgium	0.28	3	0.28	2
Germany	0.29	4	0.29	4
Luxembourg	0.31	5	0.28	2
France	0.31	5	0.29	4
Italy	0.32	7	0.31	7
Spain	0.34	8	0.32	8
Ireland	**0.34**	**8**	**0.33**	**10**
UK	0.35	10	0.32	8
Greece	0.35	10	0.34	11
Portugal	0.39	12	0.37	12

5.3 EARLIER COMPARATIVE INCOME DISTRIBUTION RESULTS

Having presented figures for Ireland's income distribution compared with other EU countries in the mid-1990s in the ECHP, it is useful to compare these with results from earlier cross-country comparative exercises. The most useful point of comparison is the comprehensive study of income inequality carried out by Atkinson, Rainwater and Smeeding (1995) for the OECD. This was based primarily on data from the Luxembourg Income Study (LIS) database and focused on surveys carried out between 1984-1988. The income concept, recipient unit and accounting period employed was similar to that used in the ECHP, the main focus being on disposable household income measured over a year without including for example imputed rent. (Unlike the ECHP, the datasets in LIS come from national surveys which are not harmonised at source: areas where data for particular countries departed from the desired measure of income or the household unit are discussed in Atkinson, Rainwater and Smeeding, Chapter 3.) They present results on the distribution of income for nine out of the eleven countries covered in this study — they did not have data for Denmark or Greece — using the square root equivalence scale and person weighting.

These can be compared with the figures presented above, and for convenience we focus in Table 5.8 on the Gini coefficient. There are major differences for some countries between the two sets of results. As summarised in the Gini coefficient, the level of inequality in the ECHP was a good deal higher than in the Atkinson, Rainwater and Smeeding (1995) results for Germany, Belgium, Luxembourg, the UK, Spain and Portugal. For the Netherlands, France, Ireland and Italy the ECHP estimates are similar to those in Atkinson *et al*. It is known from national studies that the level of income inequality did indeed rise between the mid-1980s and the mid-1990s in some EU countries, notably the UK. On this basis the increase in the UK Gini coefficient appears broadly consistent with external evidence (see, for example, Goodman, Johnson and Webb, 1997).[2] Some increase in inequality in Belgium up to 1992 is suggested by national sources (see Cantillon *et al.* 1994), but not as great as the gap between the Atkinson, Rainwater and Smeeding and ECHP figures.[3] It would, however, be surprising if the level of inequality had increased in Luxembourg and Portugal by as much as this comparison suggests, particularly when the Atkinson, Smeeding and Rainwater results for Portugal refer to 1989/90.

[2] The latter cannot be compared directly with either Atkinson *et al*. or the ECHP results because a different equivalence scale is used.

[3] Cantillon *et al.* (1994) show the Gini coefficient increasing from 0.225 in 1985 to 0.237 in 1992, using a different equivalence scale.

Table 5.8: Gini Coefficient, Equivalised Income among Persons, Square Root Scale, Wave 1 ECHP and Atkinson, Rainwater and Smeeding (ARS) Study (Equivalence scale square root of household size)

	Gini Coefficient	
	ECHP (1993)	*ARS*
Germany	0.29	0.25 (1984)
Netherlands	0.27	0.27 (1987)
Belgium	0.29	0.24 (1988)
Luxembourg	0.31	0.24 (1985)
France	0.31	0.30 (1984)
UK	0.35	0.30 (1986)
Ireland	0.34	0.33 (1987)
Italy	0.32	0.31 (1986)
Spain	0.34	0.31(1990/91)
Portugal	0.39	0.31 (1989/90)

Source: Atkinson, Rainwater and Smeeding (1995), Tables 4.3 and 4.4 except for Spain from Table 5.21 and Portugal Table 5.20.

5.4 A COMPARATIVE PERSPECTIVE ON RECENT TRENDS IN INCOME INEQUALITY

A recent study on trends in income distribution and poverty by the OECD (Forster, 2000) provides another basis of comparison for the level of inequality in Ireland versus other countries, and is also particularly valuable in terms of a comparative picture on recent trends. It does not include some of the EU countries with relatively high levels of inequality – notably Spain and Portugal – but it does include Greece, Italy and the UK. It relies on figures supplied to the OECD by national experts, including for Ireland results from the 1987 ESRI survey and the 1994 Living in Ireland survey. On this basis it shows Ireland as having about the same level of inequality as the UK in the mid-1990s, lower than Italy. However, the OECD study also shows that Ireland has a higher level of inequality than non-EU countries such as Australia and Canada, though lower than the USA. While the OECD study tried to harmonise the measurement procedures adopted across countries, differences inevitably remain; one is that while annual disposable income was the main focus, for a number of countries — including Ireland — current income had to be used. It therefore focused primarily on comparing inequality trends rather than levels.

As far as income inequality is concerned, for the ten countries for which data were available from the mid-1970s to the mid-1980s no general trends emerged, with inequality falling or stable for more countries than it was increasing. In the period from the mid-1980s to the mid-1990s, though, for which data on 20 countries was available, more of a common trend is apparent. Inequality increased in twelve countries — in half of these by considerable amounts — while it remained stable in four and decreased only slightly in another four. Ireland is shown in the study as belonging to this last group, registering a slight decrease in inequality. Several other aspects of the trends shown are worth highlighting. The UK was the only country displaying marked increases in inequality both from the mid-1970s to the mid-1980s and from the mid-1980s to the mid-1990s. The USA saw a substantial increase in inequality during the earlier period, but the OECD's figures suggest little or no further increase there by the mid-1990s. The notion that the UK's experience in particular represents a pattern which other countries will necessarily experience in time thus seems a highly partial reading of the evidence. However, the fact that the majority of countries experienced increases in inequality in the later period does clearly suggest an underlying dynamic in terms of economic forces, policy or both.

The OECD study is particularly valuable in that it goes beyond showing the extent to which trends in inequality were shared across industrialised countries, to also explore the extent to which common factors were at work. It finds some very important common features, but also many intriguing differences over the mid-1980s to mid-1990s period. Perhaps the most notable common feature is that the share of earnings going to the lower income groups among the working population decreased in all the countries covered in the study, and the share going to middle income groups generally declined as well. The same was true of market incomes generally, including income from self-employment and capital, but earnings dominate that total. This was not, or not entirely, translated into higher inequality of disposable incomes because both transfers and taxes off-set its effects, and indeed in most countries the redistributive impact of taxes and transfers increased over the period.

The declining share of earnings or market income going to lower income groups here refers to total household earnings, with households ranked by equivalised disposable income. It could reflect both changes in the distribution of earnings among earners, and in the distribution of earners across households. The OECD study does not look at the first of these in detail, being focused on households, but does have some interesting insights on the second element. It shows that the proportion of households of working age with no earner increased in most countries, and that such households had much lower levels of income than those with one or two or more earners. The proportion with two or more earners also increased in about half the countries, so there was a quite widespread tendency towards polarisation into work-rich and work-poor households. However, decomposition showed that the more important contributor to increasing inequality in household incomes was increasing inequality within fully-employed versus workless versus "mixed" households.

Another important pattern common to many of the countries covered in the study was an increase in the average incomes of the elderly towards the overall average. The main gains here were for those aged between 66 and 74 rather than those aged 75 and over, so it was recent retirees who were doing better. Also, inequality within the retirement-age population decreased in a considerable number of countries, though public old-age pensions tended to become less rather than more equally-distributed among that group reflecting the importance of earnings-related components in many countries. Non-pension transfers, on the other hand, tended to become more equally distributed among the working-age population, generally reflecting the impact of family cash benefits.

The OECD study covers the period only up to the mid-1990s, and thus does not include the period after 1994 when, as we have seen, inequality appears to have risen quite markedly in Ireland. None the less, it provides an enormously valuable comparative framework within which the Irish experience can be set, and helps to bring out some of the factors which merit further investigation in the Irish case.

5.5 CONCLUSIONS

This chapter has examined in some detail the distribution of disposable income in Ireland compared with other EU member states in the mid-1990s, using data from the European Community Household Panel survey. Ireland ranked as one of the more unequal in the European Union, along with the UK and Greece, though less so than Portugal. In the earlier study by Atkinson, Rainwater and Smeeding based on data from the mid-late 1980s, Ireland ranked among the most unequal in the OECD. The more recent data suggest rather that Ireland is one of a group of EU countries with relatively high inequality, much higher than for example Denmark. This conclusion holds when one adjusts income for differences in household size and composition using equivalence scales. The equivalence scale employed was seen to make a difference to the level of the Gini coefficient in some countries, but not the overall pattern in terms of country groupings. In particular, from an Irish perspective it does not affect the placing of Ireland in a group with the UK, Greece and Spain, having the highest level of inequality in the EU except for Portugal.

As far as international trends in income inequality are concerned, a fairly widespread though not universal trend towards increased inequality in the period from the mid-1980s to the mid-1990s is found in a recent OECD comparative study. The most notable common underlying feature noted was that the share of earnings going to the lower income groups among the working population decreased in all the countries covered in the study. This was not, or not entirely, translated into higher inequality of disposable incomes because both transfers and taxes off-set its effects, and indeed in many countries the redistributive effects of taxes and transfers increased over the period. The Irish data included in that study goes up only to 1994, but it provides a valuable comparative context in which to see the Irish experience up to that point and beyond.

Chapter 6

The Distribution of Earnings

Brian Nolan

6.1 INTRODUCTION

In this chapter we move from the distribution of income among households to the distribution of the largest element in income, namely employee's earnings, among those employees. Sharply widening inequality in earnings in the United Kingdom and the United States in the 1980s and 1990s has been a major preoccupation in recent research on inequality in those countries, and has been attributed much of the responsibility for rising inequality in the distribution of total income among households. Attempts to explain this increasing earnings dispersion have highlighted rising returns to education and skill.[1] This in turn has been attributed to a shift in demand towards more skilled labour due to factors such as skill-biased technical change (Katz and Murphy, 1992) and globalisation and competition from developing countries (Wood, 1994).[2] Some industrialised countries have experienced much smaller increases in inequality, however, while others again have maintained stability in their earnings distributions (OECD, 1993 and 1996b), which has fo-

---

[1] See for example Gosling, Machin and Meghir (1994) and Schmitt (1995) for the UK, Levy and Murnane (1992) and Juhn, Murphy and Pierce (1993) for the USA.

[2] US studies assessing such explanations include Bound and Johnson (1992), Borjas and Ramey (1994), and Burtless (1995).

cused attention on the role of institutional factors such as centralised wage bargaining.

This international context brings to the fore the need to explore the earnings distribution in Ireland and how it relates to
the structure of the overall household income distribution and
trends in that distribution. That is the aim of this chapter and the
following one. In this chapter the distribution of earnings and
how it evolved between 1987 and 1994, and again between 1994
and 1997, is analysed. Chapter 7 then looks at the relationship
between the earnings distribution and the household income
distribution, focusing on the way earners are grouped together in
households and how that has been changing as the participation
of married women in the paid labour force increases. This chapter is structured as follows. Section 6.2 describes the earnings
data to be used. Section 6.3 examines trends in the overall earnings distribution in Ireland between 1987 and 1994. Section 6.4
puts the earnings distribution in Ireland in comparative perspective. Section 6.5 looks at explanations for the observed trends in
the Irish earnings distribution between 1987 and 1994, notably
changing rates of return to different levels of education and
changes in the educational profile of the labour force. Section 6.6
summarises the conclusions.

6.2 DATA

The data to be employed come once again from the household
survey carried out by the ESRI in 1987, and the 1994 and 1997
waves of the Living in Ireland Survey. Now, rather than household income from all sources, our focus is on wages and sala-
ries. In the surveys, detailed information was obtained for employees in sample households on their earnings and hours
worked. In the 1987 survey this information covered about
2,700 employees in sample households. The corresponding
data from the 1994 Living in Ireland Survey covers over 3,000
individual employees, and in 1997 about 2,600. These samples
appear to represent all employees well when compared with
available data from the Census of Population and the Labour
Force Survey. They have served as the basis for various analyses of the extent and nature of low pay, the determinants of in-

dividual earnings, male-female wage differentials, and returns to education in Ireland.[3]

In the surveys, employees were asked about the gross pay they received in their last pay period, about income tax and PRSI contributions deducted from gross pay, about other deductions such as superannuation contributions etc., about hours worked, and about how long these particulars covered (week, fortnight, month etc.). The weekly equivalent of those current earnings (gross or after deduction of income tax and PRSI) is what enters into the calculation of total gross and disposable household income. Employees were also asked whether this was the amount they usually receive, and if not what was their usual gross and net pay and hours usually worked. In looking here at the distribution of earnings, in order to remove the effects of irregular factors such as emergency taxation, holiday pay or occasional bonuses, we use the amount usually received for about 5 per cent of respondents who stated that their last pay was not usual. As is customary in international research on the earnings distribution, we focus at this point on gross rather than after-tax earnings.

6.3 THE DISTRIBUTION OF EARNINGS IN IRELAND

In looking at the distribution of earnings across individuals, it is customary to focus on either hourly earnings, or on weekly earnings for full-time employees only. We therefore look at both the distribution of hourly earnings among all the employees in our samples, and at the distribution of weekly earnings among those working at least 30 hours per week — widely used internationally as a threshold to distinguish part-time from full-time workers. Table 6.1 shows the distribution of gross hourly and weekly earnings in Ireland in 1987, 1994 and 1997 on this basis, as measured by the bottom decile, bottom quartile, top quartile and top decile as proportions of the median.

---

[3] See for example Callan (1991b), Callan and Wren (1994), Callan and Harmon (1997), Nolan (1998), Nolan *et al* (1999).

Table 6.1: Distribution of Earnings, Ireland 1987, 1994 and 1997

As Proportion of Median	1987	1994	1997
All employees, hourly earnings:			
Bottom decile	0.47	0.47	0.48
Bottom quartile	0.73	0.68	0.69
Top quartile	1.37	1.50	1.53
Top decile	1.96	2.24	2.32
Full-time employees, weekly earnings:			
Bottom decile	0.50	0.48	0.51
Bottom quartile	0.75	0.72	0.71
Top quartile	1.35	1.43	1.42
Top decile	1.82	1.97	2.02

This shows that from 1987 to 1994 there was a consistent widening in dispersion for both weekly and hourly earnings, particularly at the top of the distribution. The ratio of the top decile to the median rises from 1.96 to 2.24 for hourly earnings, and from 1.82 to 1.97 for weekly earnings among full-time employees. For hourly earnings the bottom decile is the same proportion of the median in 1987 and in 1994, but for weekly earnings among full-time employees the bottom decile falls from 0.50 to 0.48 of the median. The ratio of the top to the bottom decile, commonly used as a single summary inequality measure in this context, rose from 4.2 to 4.8 for hourly earnings and for weekly earnings of full-time employees the increase was from 3.6 to 4.1.

Between 1994 and 1997, the top decile continued to move further away from the median, reaching 2.32 for hourly earnings. In the bottom half of the distribution, however, the bottom decile now kept pace with the median, if anything increasing marginally faster. As a result, the ratio of the top to the bottom decile was unchanged at 4.8 for hourly earnings, and marginally down at 4.0 for weekly earnings among full-time workers.

Over the whole period from 1987 to 1997, then, there was a substantial widening in earnings dispersion in terms of hourly wages among all employees. This was more pronounced in the

1987-94 period than from 1994 on, so rapid economic growth did not lead to an acceleration in the trend. It was primarily driven by relatively rapid increases for those towards the top of the distribution, with no indication – unlike for example the UK or the USA – that the bottom was falling behind the median.

6.4 IRELAND'S EARNINGS DISTRIBUTION IN COMPARATIVE PERSPECTIVE

A comparative perspective on the Irish earnings distribution, and on the way it has been changing, can be obtained using measures of earnings dispersion for a range of developed countries brought together by the OECD (1996b). There are potentially important differences in definition and coverage across countries (including whether earnings are weekly or annual), so these comparisons should be treated with extreme care, but they can serve to highlight some key features of the Irish results. Since they cover only up to the mid-1990s, we use the Irish figures for 1994 and for trends between 1987-1994 for comparative purposes.

First, Table 6.2 shows measures of the level of earnings dispersion in 1994 for Ireland and other OECD countries, for weekly pay among full-time employees (since the figures brought together by the OECD generally refer to full-time employees, and to weekly, monthly or annual rather than hourly gross earnings). Ireland is seen to have a particularly high level of earnings dispersion. Both the ratio of the top decile to the median and of the median to the bottom decile are among the highest of the countries covered. With the top decile/bottom decile summary measure, only Canada and the USA are seen to have greater earnings inequality than Ireland.

As far as trends in earnings dispersion are concerned, Table 6.3 shows the ratio of the top to the bottom decile in 1987 and 1994 for Ireland and the other OECD countries for which the figures are available for both points in time. We see that once again Ireland is an outlier: the increase in earnings dispersion is the greatest of any of the countries shown. (The US is not included in this table because OECD 1996 gives only US figures for men and women separately, but from these it appears that the increase in earnings dispersion in the USA over the period may be similar in scale to that seen for Ireland.)

Table 6.2: Summary Measures of Earnings Dispersion, Ireland and Other OECD countries, 1994

	Top Decile/Median	Median/Bottom Decile	Top/Bottom Decile
Sweden	1.59*	1.34*	2.13
Belgium*	1.57	1.43	2.24
Germany*	1.61	1.44	2.32
Finland	1.70	1.40	2.38
Netherlands	1.66	1.56	2.59
Switzerland	1.68	1.58	2.65
Italy*	1.60	1.75	2.80
Australia	1.75	1.64	2.87
Japan	1.85	1.63	3.02
New Zealand	1.76	1.73	3.05
France	1.99	1.65	3.28
UK	1.86	1.78	3.31
Austria	1.82	2.01	3.66
Canada	1.84	2.28	4.20
US	2.07	2.10	4.35
Ireland	**1.97**	**2.06**	**4.06**

* = 1993

Source: OECD (1996b), Table 3.1, p. 61-62, and Table 6.1 above.

Table 6.3: Trends in Earnings Dispersion, Ireland and Other OECD Countries, 1987-1994

	Top Decile/Bottom Decile		
	1987	*1994*	*Change*
Canada**	4.44	4.20	-0.24
Germany*	2.54	2.32	-0.22
Belgium*	2.44	2.24	-0.20
Finland	2.52	2.38	-0.14
Japan	3.15	3.02	-0.13
Sweden	2.09	2.13	0.04
Australia	2.81	2.87	0.06
Netherlands	2.53	2.59	0.06
France	3.19	3.28	0.09
UK	3.20	3.31	0.11
New Zealand**	2.92	3.05	0.13
Austria	3.47	3.66	0.19
Italy*	2.42	2.80	0.38
Ireland	**3.67**	**4.06**	**0.39**

* = 1993 not 1994; ** = 1988 not 1987.

Source: OECD (1996b), Table 3.1, p. 61-62, and Table 6.1 above.

6.5 EXPLAINING THE INCREASE IN EARNINGS INEQUALITY

We have seen that the dispersion in earnings among employees in Ireland is high by international standards, and rose relatively rapidly between 1987 and 1994. From 1994 to 1997 the earnings distribution was rather more stable, though the top did continue to draw away from the middle. We now attempt to identify factors that may have been driving the increase in earnings inequality, concentrating on the 1987-1994 period and drawing on results presented in Barrett, Callan and Nolan (1999).

As mentioned earlier, sharply widening inequality in earnings in the United Kingdom and the United States in the 1980s and 1990s has been attributed to rising returns to education and skill. This in turn has been attributed to factors such as skill-biased technical change and globalisation and competition from developing countries. Here we look at returns to education and changes in the educational profile of employees in the Irish case, and the extent to which this may have contributed to increasing earnings dispersion. The fact that this increase in earnings inequality has not been experienced to anything like the same extent in some other industrialised countries has also focused attention on the role of institutional factors such as centralised wage bargaining and minimum wage legislation. We therefore also point to some relevant features of the Irish institutional background.

During the 1980s and into the 1990s, there has been a rapid rise in the level of educational attainment of those leaving the Irish education system. This reflects substantially higher numbers completing full second-level education rather than leaving early, and a marked increase in the proportion going on to third-level education. As cohorts containing a high proportion with relatively low levels of education retire and those with relatively high levels enter the labour force, this has produced the rather dramatic change in the education profile of employees between 1987 and 1994 shown in Table 6.4. Whereas in 1987, 28 per cent of employees did not have a formal qualification beyond primary level, by 1994 this had fallen to 17 per cent. This was accompanied by a rise in the percentage with post-secondary school attainment levels from 18 per cent to 24 per cent. We now go on to explore the relationship between this changing education profile and the distribution of earnings.

Table 6.4: Education Attainment Level, Ireland 1987 and 1994

Highest Qualification Achieved	1987 (%)	1994 (%)
Primary only	28.0	16.9
Junior cycle	24.7	23.2
Leaving Cert.	29.7	35.5
Certificate/Diploma	7.6	8.7
Degree	10.0	15.7
All	100.0	100.0

Table 6.5 looks first at median earnings by education category and how this evolved between 1987 and 1994. The greatest percentage increase over the period was for those with university degrees, for whom the median rose by 52 per cent, compared with 30-38 per cent for the other attainment levels. The table also looks at dispersion within education categories, in terms of the ratio of the top to the bottom decile. This measure shows that the degree of dispersion was widest within the post-school non-degree category in each year, but rose considerably within the bottom and the top education categories between 1987 and 1994.

Table 6.5: Median Hourly Earnings and Ratio of Top to Bottom Decile by Education Category, All Employees, 1987 and 1994 (IR£ per hour)

	Median	Median	% Increase	Top Decile/ Bottom Decile	
	1987	*1994*		*1987*	*1994*
Primary only	3.75	5.00	33.3	2.73	3.16
Junior cycle	3.83	5.28	37.9	3.44	3.86
Leaving Certificate	4.35	5.68	30.6	3.80	3.76
Diploma/other third level	5.48	7.23	32.9	4.56	4.73
Degree	8.40	12.78	52.1	3.23	3.90
All	4.30	5.98	39.1	4.16	4.77

With the balance between men and women in the workforce changing, it is also interesting to look at male and female employees separately. The educational profile of male and female employees changed in very much the same way as that for all employees. Although a higher proportion of men than women had only primary-level qualifications, this declined very rapidly for both, and the percentage with post-school qualifications also rose substantially for both men and women. The relatively rapid increase in median hourly earnings between 1987 and 1994 for those with university degrees was also seen both among men and women, and the same is true of the considerable increase in dispersion within that education category between 1987 and 1994.

It is also instructive to look within particular age ranges. Focusing on employees aged 25-39, once again there was a substantial shift in educational profile between 1987 and 1994. The percentage with only primary-level qualifications fell from 23 per cent to only 9 per cent for this sub-set, and the percentage with a university degree rose to 16 per cent. The higher levels of educational attainment again show a relatively rapid rate of increase in median earnings. The overall dispersion in hourly earnings has risen for this age range though more modestly than for all employees, with the ratio of the top to the bottom decile going from 3.1 to 3.3. Dispersion has increased within most education groups, with the largest increase again for those with university degrees.

Such analyses of trends in earnings of employees cross-classified by sex, age and education category are useful, but the influence of different factors, notably returns to education, can be distinguished more easily using estimated earnings equations. The extent to which wage premia for different educational qualifications changed over the period has been investigated using that approach in Barrett, Callan and Nolan (1999). Using the 1987 and 1994 datasets, standard human capital wage equations, based on educational qualifications and a number of other relevant characteristics, were estimated for both years. The general picture revealed by the results is one of increased returns to university degrees and to the junior cycle qualifications, with approximate stability for the returns to the Leaving Certificate. There was also some evidence of a slight decline in returns to non-university third level qualifications. Barrett, Callan and Nolan also analyse the extent to which this pattern of changes in returns to education, and changes in the age-education profile of employees, explains the increase in wage dispersion between 1987 and 1994. The results depend to some extent on the precise specification of the wage equation and other aspects of the decomposition methodology employed. They show that much of the total increase in dispersion at the top of the distribution (measured by the ratio of the top decile to the median) is explained by the changes in rates of return to education alone. Taken together, the combination of the change in the age-education profile of employees and higher returns to education account for most of the observed increase in dispersion in earnings between 1987 and 1994.

The scale of the increase in earnings dispersion in Ireland compared with the US and the UK is particularly striking in the light of the very different approaches to labour market institutions adopted in these countries. The UK and US have been archetypes of flexible labour markets, with minimal state regulation, decentralised wage bargaining systems and low and falling levels of social security floors for labour market participants. Precisely since 1987, as it happens, Ireland has operated a "social partnership approach". This has involved national agreements on wage levels in both private and public sectors, together with agreement between the state, employers, trade unions and farming interests on a wide range of economic and social policies including tax reform, welfare payments, and labour law. Trade union membership declined during the 1980s but remains relatively high. At a time when Wages Councils were being abolished in the UK, the wage minima set by Ireland's Joint Labour Committees continued to rise in line with earnings over the period. There was also a substantial expansion in the numbers covered with the introduction of a Joint Labour Committee for the retail sector in 1993.

The evolution relative to earnings of the safety-net support provided by social security payments for the unemployed also offers a striking contrast between Ireland and the UK over the period. In 1987, this support represented a similar proportion of average earnings in the two countries — about 50 per cent for a couple with three children, for example. However, means-tested support rates in Ireland rose a good deal more rapidly than earnings to 1994, whereas in the UK they lagged behind earnings substantially. The result was that by 1994 the corresponding figures for a couple with three children were 60 per cent for Ireland and 43 per cent in the UK (Callan and Sutherland, 1997). In the light of these contrasts in institutional background between Ireland and the UK, much remains to be understood about the rapidly rising dispersion in earnings in Ireland between 1987 and 1994.

6.6 Conclusions

This chapter has used data from household surveys to examine
the distribution of earnings among Irish employees in 1987,
1994 and 1997. The results show that the dispersion in the Irish
earnings distribution was relatively high by international standards in 1994, and that it increased between 1987 and 1994 by
more than in almost any other OECD country for which data are
available. This increase in dispersion was pronounced at the
top of the distribution, and was seen for hourly earnings among
all employees and for weekly earnings among full-time employees. Estimated wage equations showed that returns to
higher levels of education, especially university education, increased over the period. Taken together, the combination of
the change in the age-education profile of employees and
higher returns to education account for much of the observed
increase in dispersion, though precisely how much depends on
the specification of the wage equation and other aspects of the
decomposition methodology employed. Between 1994 and
1997, when economic growth accelerated rapidly, the increase
in earnings inequality slowed although the top of the distribution did continue to move away from the middle.

Chapter 7

Female Labour Force Participation and Household Income Inequality in Ireland

Donal O'Neill and Olive Sweetman

7.1 INTRODUCTION

One of the most notable changes in the Irish labour market in recent years has been the rapid growth in the number of women working outside the home, in the paid labour force. In this chapter we examine the relationship between this trend and the distribution of income among households. While the scale and nature of women's labour force participation can have a substantial impact on the household income distribution, it is not obvious *a priori* what this impact will be. Depending on how much those women earn, and on the type of household from which they come, an increase in women's labour force participation could be equalising or disequalising in terms of the household income distribution. We therefore explore empirically what the impact is likely to have been in the Irish case, using the period 1987-94 for this purpose. Section 7.2 describes the data we use to carry out the analysis, Section 7.3 provides a detailed description of changes in female participation rates in a household setting, and estimates the contribution these changes have had on household income inequality. Section 7.4 presents conclusions.

7.2 WOMEN'S LABOUR FORCE PARTICIPATION IN IRELAND

To see the Irish situation in comparative context, Table 7.1 shows female participation rates for various OECD countries in both 1984 and 1994. In 1984 the female labour force participation rate in Ireland was 37 per cent. In contrast, many of the other countries had female participation rates of over 50 per cent. For instance, the participation rate in the US was approximately 63 per cent, 59 per cent in the U.K, 53 per cent in Germany and 77 per cent in Sweden. Of the OECD countries in the table, only Spain had a lower participation rate than Ireland. By 1994 the participation rate in Ireland had increased to 47 per cent. Table 7.1 shows that of the OECD countries for which data are available only four — Luxembourg, Netherlands, New Zealand and Spain — experienced greater percentage increases in the female participation rate than Ireland. These increases in participation and employment have continued since 1994. Indeed, the employment increases among Irish women between 1991 and 1997 exceeded the combined employment increases over the previous 20 years. Many have argued that this has contributed substantially to Ireland's impressive growth record since the early 1990's (see for example Bradley, FitzGerald, Honohan and Kearney 1997).

To understand the effect of increasing female participation on household income inequality, one needs information showing where in the income distribution these changes have been occurring, and also what has been happening to female wages as women's participation and employment increased. For this purpose we use the two household surveys carried out by the ESRI in 1987 and 1994, described in detail in earlier chapters. The unit of analysis at this point is the household. However, to focus on the role of female participation we concentrate on households containing a married couple in which both spouses are present and both are aged between 24 and 55. This leaves us with 1,546 households in 1987, and 1,855 households in 1994.

Table 7.1: Female Participation Rates in the OECD, 1984 and 1994

Country	Female Participation Rate (%)		Change in Participation Rate (% points)
	1984	*1994*	
Australia	52.8	63.4	+20
Austria	51.5	62.1	+20
Belgium	48.7	55.1	+13
Canada	63.5	67.8	+7
Denmark	73.8	73.8	0
Finland	72.9	69.9	-5
France	54.7	59.6	+8
Germany	52.3	61.8	+18
Greece	40.9	44.6	+9
Iceland	62.7	80.0	+28
Ireland	**36.9**	**47.2**	**+28**
Italy	40.7	42.9	+6
Japan	57.2	62.1	+9
Korea	43.8	52.7	+20
Luxembourg	42.2	56.5	+34
Netherlands	40.7	57.4	+41
New Zealand	46.0	65.0	+41
Norway	66.3	71.1	+7
Portugal	56.0	62.0	+11
Spain	33.2	44.1	+33
Sweden	77.3	74.4	-4
Switzerland	55.7	67.5	+21
UK	59.1	66.2	+12
US	62.8	70.5	+12

Focusing on these households, between the two surveys there was a significant increase in the percentage of married women working as employees. In 1987 approximately 22 per cent of wives were classified as employees, but by 1994 this had increased to 34 per cent. It is useful now to distinguish between four sources of household income: husband's employee earn-

ings, wife's earnings, other earnings (accruing to other household members) and all other income (income from self-
employed income (including farming), from capital, occupational pensions, and state transfers). We see from Table 7.2 that
the increase in employment rates for women was also reflected
in the share of household income accounted for by female
earnings, which increased from under 12 per cent of total gross
household income in 1987 to 15 per cent in 1994. In the next
section we examine these trends in more detail and in particular their impact on household income inequality, with this categorisation of income allowing us to highlight the role of wives'
earnings versus other income sources.

**Table 7.2: Components of Gross Household Income (house-
holds with couples aged 24-55) 1987-1994**

	Share of Total Household Income (%)	
	1987	*1994*
Man's earnings	50.3	47.8
Woman's earnings	11.7	15.0
Earnings of others	7.6	8.2
Other income	30.3	29.0

7.3 FEMALE LABOUR SUPPLY AND HOUSEHOLD INEQUALITY

We saw in the previous chapter that the distribution of earnings
among all Irish employees became more widely dispersed
between 1987 and 1994. This was also true for the married men
employees in the sub-sample of households on whom we are now
focusing. Their ratio of top to bottom decile (weekly earnings)
went up from 2.9 to 3.3.[1] For married women employees, dispersion also went up. This is in contrast to the trend in total household income inequality for the sub-sample, which has fallen

---

[1] Although the results are presented here for the ratio of the top decile to the
bottom decile of the earnings distribution the same conclusions hold when we
use alternative measures such as the Gini coefficient or Atkinson's measure of
inequality.

slightly over this period, consistent with the pattern described in Chapter 4 for the entire sample.

The relationship between the participation and wages of women and their husbands' economic status will clearly have an important role to play in determining patterns of household inequality. Table 7.3 shows that the strength of the association between the husband's and the wife's earnings, as summarised by the correlation between them, increased substantially over this period.

Table 7.3: Correlation between Earnings of Married Couples, 1987 and 1994

Correlation between Husband and Wife's Weekly Earnings	1987	1994
All Households	0.05	0.12
Households with Working Wives	0.03	0.14

To examine what lay behind this change, we can first look at which women moved into employment, in terms of their husband's labour force status and position in the earnings distribution. Table 7.4 shows that in 1987 employment rates (i.e. the percentage working as an employee) were higher for women married to husbands with earnings in the top half of the earnings distribution than those on lower earnings. However, it also shows that while wives' employment rates increased throughout the male earnings distribution, the bulk of the change in employment rates was concentrated among women married to men with below average earnings. The only ones not to experience an increase in employment rates were women married to unemployed men, whose employment rate fell from 20 per cent to 17 per cent.[2] As mentioned in Chapter 5, such a concentration of employment in work-rich versus work-poor households has been noted in various countries.

---

[2] For more information on the labour supply behaviour of women married to unemployed men see Doris (1998).

Table 7.4: Female Employment Rate by Male Earnings, 1987-1994

Husband's Position in Earnings Distribution	Female Employment Rate		% Change 1987-1994
	1987	*1994*	
Husband an employee in the			
First Decile	24.6	30.8	+25
Second Decile	16.6	45.7	+175
Third Decile	18.6	45.0	+141
Fourth Decile	20.8	43.7	+110
Fifth Decile	17.8	43.2	+143
Sixth Decile	26.7	47.5	+78
Seventh Decile	19.0	42.0	+121
Eight Decile	28.3	42.9	+52
Ninth Decile	31.7	38.1	+20
Tenth Decile	23.4	28.5	+22
Below Median	19.4	41.7	+115
Above Median	25.7	39.8	+55
Husband unemployed	*20.1*	*16.7*	*-17*

This change in the pattern of female employment might in itself be expected to reduce household income inequality. To get a complete picture of the contribution of female earnings to household income inequality, though, we also need to know what was happening to the level of earnings of women in different households over the 1987-1994 period. Compared to the way participation rates have evolved, this in fact reveals a very different story. The greatest wage increase was among working women married to men with above average earnings, for whom real wages increased by 17 per cent. In contrast, for women married to men with below average earnings, real wages increased by only 2 per cent. Women employees married to unemployed men actually saw their real weekly wage fall over this period (though this is based on relatively few observations).[3]

---

[3] One needs to be careful in interpreting the wage figure for women married to unemployed men as the estimates are imprecise. This reflects the small

These wage changes contributed substantially to the increase in the correlation between spouses' earnings over the period.

If the growth in part-time work was more prevalent among workers at the lower end of the distribution, the fall in real weekly wages for women married to unemployed men could then simply reflect an increasing proportion of these workers working shorter weeks. However, the same pattern emerges when we look at hourly wages, with the real hourly wage for women married to high-earning husbands going up 30 per cent, compared to 9 per cent for women married to low earning husbands and once again a decline for women married to unemployed men. The female earnings distribution itself became more unequal, with the ratio of the top to bottom decile of the female wage distribution increasing from 9.3 to 10.4 between 1987 and 1994.[4] The impact of increasing participation means that if we look at all wives, by contrast, we see a reduction in dispersion because there are significantly fewer with no earnings at all.

This analysis identifies two channels whereby recent trends in female labour supply and wages would have worked to actually increase household income inequality. The first is that the wage growth among females has been most pronounced among women married to high earning husbands, so the correlation between male and female wages has increased. This increased correlation would tend to increase household income dispersion, other things fixed. Secondly, the distribution of female wages tends to be much more dispersed than that of male workers. As female earnings becomes a more important part of household income the greater dispersion exhibited within the distribution of female earnings will tend to feed into the distribution of household income. The changing pattern of female

---

sample sizes on which the wage changes for this category of worker are calculated.

[4] A possible explanation for the faster increase in earnings among women married to men with above average earnings is the increase in returns to education which have occurred over this period in Ireland, as described in Chapter 6. Given the tendency for couples of similar education levels to marry we might expect the rise in return to skill to be reflected in faster earnings growth for women married to high income men.

employment, on the other hand, with a greater increase in employment for women with low-earning rather than high-earning husbands, might in itself be expected to reduce household income inequality.

It is interesting to contrast the Irish experience with what has been happening in the US, where Juhn and Murphy (1997) examined changes in female earnings and employment between 1969 and 1989. Their analysis shows that the trend in female wage behaviour in the US is similar to Ireland, with the largest gains being experienced by women married to high earning husbands. However, the employment behaviour over the period is the opposite of what we have just seen for Ireland: the highest employment rates were initially found among women married to low income men, but over time the largest increases in employment have been among women married to high earning husbands. Thus, in the US both the wage change effects and the participation effects for females operated in such a way as to result in an increase in household income inequality. As we have shown for Ireland these forces operated in opposite directions between 1987 and 1994, and we must turn to a more detailed analysis in order to determine which of the two had the greater bearing on inequality.

Total household income can be disaggregated into its components in order to determine their individual impacts on inequality, allowing us to identify the effect of wives' earnings and employment on inequality and how it has been changing. The coefficient of variation is a summary inequality measure which is particularly suited to this purpose, and we have used it to look at the period from 1987 to 1994: the details of the methodology and results are shown in Appendix 1. The results suggest that, despite the fact that the correlation in spouses' earnings has increased substantially over this period, the evolution of wives' earnings had an equalising effect on the distribution of household income in Ireland over this period. The increased correlation between the earnings of spouses would in itself have had a disequalising effect. However, its impact was outweighed by the reduction in dispersion in earnings across all married women (as the numbers employed increased), and by a reduction in the correlation between wives' earnings and non-labour income. This brings out the complexity of the relationships between individual and household incomes, and the need to carefully disaggregate the different sources of income accruing to household members and the ways in which they relate to each other.

7.4 CONCLUSION

Between 1987 and 1994 wage inequality in Ireland increased substantially yet household income inequality, as reflected in the ESRI surveys carried out in those years, was stable or actually fell marginally. In this chapter we have examined one possible explanation for this, namely the increased contribution of female wages to total household income. We have documented the changes in wives' employment rates and earnings over this period, paying particular attention to how these varied with the economic status of the husband.

We saw that while increases in female employment rates were greatest among wives married to low earning husbands, these women have experienced only modest wage gains when compared to the wives of husbands with earnings above the average. These changes have resulted in a reduction in the dispersion of earnings among all wives (the participation effect) but an increase in dispersion among wives at work and an increase in the correlation between spouses' earnings (both wage effects).

We then used a decomposition of the coefficient of variation, a summary measure of inequality, to examine the contribution of wives' earnings to changes in household income inequality over the period. The results suggest that the effect of the higher correlation in spouses' earnings (which would in itself work to increase inequality) was dominated by the other trends associated with wives' earnings. Overall, changes in wives' earnings would have had an equalising rather than disequalising impact on household incomes over the period.

Although we have shown that trends in female participation rates have reduced income inequality over the 1987-94 period, one must be careful in extrapolating these findings from that point on. Despite the rapid increases in female participation, female earnings still accounted for only 15 per cent of total household income in 1994. Given the continued increase in women's labour force participation, this share is set to grow in importance and as it does one would expect the relative importance of female-specific factors for household inequality will also increase.

Chapter 8

Conclusions

Brian Nolan

Overall income inequality and inequality in the distribution of earnings have risen sharply during the 1980s and 1990s in a number of industrialised countries, giving rise to widespread concern about the factors at work and about the societal implications. This makes it particularly important to know how the distribution of income in Ireland has been changing over time, how it compares with other countries, and what factors contribute to explaining Ireland's particular experience. This study has addressed these questions, using household survey data.

These data allowed us to first provide a picture of the distribution of household income in Ireland in 1994, 1997 and 1998, then to compare these with similar figures for 1987 and earlier years. These figures for Ireland were also compared with estimates for other countries. The evolution of the distribution of earnings among individual earners, a major factor behind increasing inequality elsewhere, was analysed. Finally, the impact of changes in the extent of women's participation in the paid labour force was assessed.

A key finding from the analysis of data for the 1990s from the Living in Ireland surveys was that there was a marked shift in the disposable income distribution away from the bottom 30 per cent. Over the period from 1994 to 1998, and adjusting income for differences in household size and composition, the share of the bottom 30 per cent of households declined by 1.4 per cent of total income.

The distribution among households of income coming directly from the market did not become more unequal over the period; instead, an important factor was that social welfare transfers, though having an equalising effect in each year, had more impact in 1994. The period between 1994 and 1997 also saw a considerable change in composition both at the top and bottom of the distribution, with younger households moving up and older ones moving down.

Over the period from 1973-87, on the other hand, inequality in the distribution of disposable household income fell markedly, with the share of the top decile down by 1.4 per cent of total income and that of the bottom quintile up by 0.9 per cent. The share of the top decile fell both from 1973 to 1980 and from 1980 to 1987, but the increase for the bottom decile was in the latter period. An important factor at work over this period was the increasingly redistributive impact of income tax and employees' social insurance contributions, reflecting both an increase in progressivity and a very substantial rise in the average tax rate. From 1987 to 1994 this continued but at a much slower rate, helping to explain the greater stability in the shape of the distribution over those years.

Using data from the European Community Household Panel Survey, Ireland had one of the more unequal income distributions in the EU in the mid-1990s. In the earlier study by Atkinson *et al*, based on data from the mid-late 1980s, Ireland ranked among the most unequal in the OECD. The more recent data suggest rather that Ireland is one of a group of EU countries – the others being the UK, Greece and Spain - with relatively high inequality, though not as high as Portugal. This conclusion holds when one adjusts income for differences in household size and composition using equivalence scales. The equivalence scale employed was seen to make a difference to the level of the Gini coefficient in some countries, but not to the overall pattern in terms of country groupings.

As far as international trends in income inequality are concerned, a fairly widespread though not universal trend towards increased inequality in the period from the mid-1980s to the mid-1990s was found in a recent OECD comparative study. The most notable common underlying feature noted was that the share of earnings going to the lower income groups among the working population decreased in all the countries covered in the study. This was not, or not entirely, translated into higher inequality of disposable incomes because both transfers and taxes off-set its effects, and indeed in many countries the redistributive effects of taxes and transfers increased over the period.

Data from the ESRI household surveys was also used to examine the distribution of earnings among Irish employees in 1987, 1994 and 1997. The dispersion in Irish earnings was relatively high by international standards in 1994, having increased from 1987 by more than most other OECD countries for which data are available. The combination of changes in the age-education profile of employees and higher returns to education accounted for much of that increase in dispersion. Between 1994 and 1997, when Irish economic growth accelerated rapidly, the increase in earnings inequality slowed although the top of the distribution did continue to move away from the middle.

The participation of married women in the paid labour force has been increasing rapidly in Ireland, so their wages have been accounting for a growing proportion of household income. Elsewhere, this has been seen to increase household income inequality. That was found not to be the case for Ireland between 1987 and 1994, indeed the overall impact of increased participation was seen to have an equalising effect. This was mostly because increases in female employment rates were greatest among wives married to husbands with relatively low earnings. There is no guarantee that this has continued to be the case as married women's labour force participation has continued to rise, but this finding serves to demonstrate the complexity of the relationship between trends in the labour market and the household income distribution.

Much remains to be done before we fully understand how the shape of the Irish income distribution has been evolving and the nature of the forces producing that distribution. This study should be seen as providing one of the building-blocks on which such an understanding can be built.

Appendix 1

Decomposition of Total Household Income Inequality by Factor Components, 1987-1994

Chapter 7 made reference to results from the disaggregation of total household income into its individual components in order to identify the effect of wives earnings and employment on inequality. This appendix sets out the details of the decomposition methodology employed and the results.[1]

The issues associated with decomposing total inequality by income components are examined in Shorrocks (1982a,b). He shows that by appropriate choice of a weighting function one can find alternative decompositions of a given inequality index which yield vastly different conclusions concerning the importance of a given component. In fact, the contribution of any factor expressed as a proportion of total inequality can be made to take any value between plus and minus infinity. Furthermore, he shows that there are no strong statistical reasons for choosing any one of these decompositions over the other. Shorrocks argues that a potential means of choosing between the multiplicity of outcomes is to focus on what is normally meant by statements of the form "factor X contributes Z percent of total inequality".

Canican and Reed (1998) develop this idea further by comparing two common inequality indices, the coefficient of variation and the Gini coefficient. They argue that the standard de-

---

[1] For other studies using a similar approach to examining income inequality see Layard and Zabalza (1979), Canican, Danzinger and Gottschalk (1993) and Machin and Waldfogel (1994).

composition of the Gini coefficient has no implicit reference distribution and therefore should not be interpreted as a measure of the effect of an income source on inequality, and that decompositions based on the Gini coefficient are not suitable to analysing changes in inequality over time. They analyse such changes using the coefficient of variation, developing several "thought experiments". Here this approach is applied to the contribution of wives' earnings to household income inequality between 1987 and 1994.

The first experiment was to compare the observed inequality in household incomes in 1987 to the inequality that would have been seen if the distribution of wives' earnings had changed to the 1994 pattern, but all other income components had stayed fixed at their 1987 levels. The second experiment was to compare the actual distribution in 1994 with what the level of inequality would have been if wives' earnings had stayed at their 1987 levels. The results using these two alternative counterfactuals may differ because the base year values differ between the two — a common problem in other areas, for example using base-year versus end-year weights in constructing index numbers. As in those contexts, here we derive both sets of results and see if they show the same broad pattern. The results for both decompositions are given in Table A1.1.

Table A1.1: Decomposition of Changes in the Coefficient of Variation for Gross Household Income, 1987-1994

	Coefficient of Variation
Observed 1987	0.678
1987 with women's earnings at 1994 levels	0.671/0.663*
1994 with women's earnings at 1987 levels	0.656/0.662*
Observed 1994	0.644

* The exact figure depends on the assumption about changes in the correlations between income sources.

These results suggest that, despite the fact that the correlation in spouses' earnings has increased substantially over this period, the evolution of wives' earnings had an equalising effect on the distribution of household income. The reduction in dispersion in earnings across all married women (reflecting increasing numbers employed), as well as a reduction in the correlation between wives' earnings and non-labour income, were equalising in terms of the household income distribution. These were large enough to outweigh the effect of the increased correlation between the earnings of spouses, which in itself would have worked in the opposite direction.

Appendix 2

Table A2.1: Decile Shares in Equivalised Disposable Income for Irish Households, 1994 and 1997 LII Surveys (1/0.66/0.33 Scale)

	Share in Total Equivalised (1/0.66/0.33) Disposable Income (%)	
Decile	*1994 LII*	*1997 LII*
Bottom	3.9	3.6
2	4.8	4.6
3	5.4	5.2
4	6.1	6.1
5	7.1	7.5
6	8.7	9.0
7	10.5	10.7
8	12.7	13.0
9	15.9	15.9
Top	25.0	24.6
All	100.0	100.0
Inequality Measure		
Gini	0.326	0.329
Theil	0.184	0.185

Table A2.2: Position in the Income Distribution of Persons Categorised by Age of Household Head, 1994 and 1997 LII Surveys

Quintile	Position in Equivalised (1/0.66/0.33) Disposable Income Distribution (%)		
	Head Aged under 35	Head Aged 35-64	Head Aged 65 or Over
A: 1994			
Bottom	26.5	20.4	9.9
2	11.3	18.0	41.3
3	14.9	20.6	22.0
4	21.0	21.4	13.2
Top	26.2	19.7	13.6
All	100.0	100.0	100.0
B: 1997			
Bottom	18.4	19.9	22.0
2	12.2	19.2	33.7
3	18.6	21.0	16.9
4	19.4	20.6	18.8
Top	31.5	19.3	8.6
All	100.0	100.0	100.0

Table A2.3: Position in the Income Distribution of Persons Categorised by Labour Force Status of Household Head, 1994 LII Survey

Quintile	Position in Equivalised (1/0.66/0.33) Disposable Income Distribution (%)					
	Employee	*Self-employed*	*Farmer*	*Unemployed*	*Retired*	*Home duties*
A: 1994						
Bottom	4.5	17.4	22.7	61.6	10.2	32.8
2	10.0	11.0	17.2	24.6	33.3	43.0
3	23.0	21.3	23.4	9.4	26.1	12.5
4	31.1	20.8	19.9	3.3	15.3	7.3
Top	31.5	29.4	16.8	1.1	15.0	4.4
All	100.0	100.0	100.0	100.0	100.0	100.0
B: 1997						
Bottom	4.7	16.7	17.6	68.0	15.7	46.4
2	12.5	14.4	25.0	24.8	30.9	36.1
3	25.0	15.7	24.2	4.5	18.6	10.9
4	28.4	18.2	17.3	2.2	22.3	5.0
Top	29.3	35.0	15.9	0.5	12.5	1.6
All	100.0	100.0	100.0	100.0	100.0	100.0

References

Atkinson, A.B., L. Rainwater and T. M. Smeeding (1995). *Income Distribution in OECD Countries: Evidence from the Luxembourg Income Study*, Paris: OECD.

Barrett, A., T. Callan and B. Nolan (1999). "Returns to Education in the Irish Youth Labour Market", *Journal of Population Economics* Vol. 12, 313-326.

Borjas, G. and V. Ramey (1994). "Time-Series Evidence on the Sources of Trends in Wage Inequality", *American Economic Review,* Papers and Proceedings, 84, 10-16.

Bound, J. and G. Johnson (1992). "Changes in the Structure of Wages During the 1980s: An Evaluation of Alternative Explanations", *American Economic Review*, 82, 371-92.

Bradley, J., J. FitzGerald, P. Honohan, and I. Kearney (1997). "Interpreting the Recent Irish Growth Experience", in Duffy, D., J. FitzGerald, I. Kearney and F. Shortall, (eds*.), Medium-Term Review: 1997-2003*, Dublin: The Economic and Social Research Institute.

Buhman, B., L. Rainwater, G. Schmaus and T. Smeeding (1988). "Equivalence Scales, Well-being, Inequality and Poverty: Sensitivity Estimates Across Ten Countries Using the Luxembourg Income Study Database", *Review of Income and Wealth*, Series 34: 115-42.

Burtless, G. (1995). "International Trade and the Rise in Earnings Inequality", *Journal of Economic Literature*, 33(2), 800-816.

Callan, T. (1991a). *Income Tax and Welfare Reform: Microsimulation Modelling and Analysis*, General Research Series No. 154, Dublin: The Economic and Social Research Institute.

Callan, T. (1991b). "Male-Female Wage Differentials in Ireland", *Economic and Social Review*, 23, 55-72.

Callan, T. and C. Harmon (1997). *The Economic Return to Schooling in Ireland*, Department of Economics Working Paper WP97/23, Dublin: University College.

Callan, T., R. Layte, B. Nolan, D. Watson, C.T. Whelan, J. Williams and B. Maître (1999). *Monitoring Poverty Trends*, Dublin: Stationery Office.

Callan, T. and B. Nolan (1994). "Unemployment and Poverty", in B. Nolan and T. Callan (eds), *Poverty and Policy in Ireland*, Dublin: Gill and Macmillan.

Callan, T. and B. Nolan (1997). "Income Inequality and Poverty in Ireland in the 1970s and 1980s," in Gottschalk, P., B. Gustafsson and E. Palmer (eds.)*The Distribution of Economic Welfare in the 1980s: An International Perspective*, Cambridge: Cambridge University Press.

Callan, T. and B. Nolan (1999). "Income Inequality in Ireland in the 1980s and 1990s," in F. Barry (ed.) *Understanding Ireland's Economic Growth*, Basingstoke: Macmillan.

Callan, T., B. Nolan, and B.J. Whelan, D.F. Hannan, with S. Creighton (1989). *Poverty, Income and Welfare in Ireland*, General Research Series No. 146, Dublin: The Economic and Social Research Institute.

Callan, T., B. Nolan, B.J. Whelan, C.T. Whelan and J. Williams (1996). *Poverty in the 1990s: Evidence from the 1994 Living in Ireland Survey*, Dublin: Oak Tree Press.

Callan, T. and H. Sutherland (1997). "Income Supports in Ireland and the UK", in T. Callan (ed.), *Income Support and Work Incentives: Ireland and the UK,* Policy Research Series Paper No. 30, Dublin: The Economic and Social Research Institute.

Callan, T. and A. Wren (1994). *Male-Female Wage Differentials: Analysis and Policy Issues,* General Research Series Paper No. 163, Dublin: The Economic and Social Research Institute.

Cantillon, S. and B. Nolan (1998). "Are Married Women More Deprived than their Husbands?", *Journal of Social Policy*, 27, 2, 151-171.

Cantillon, S. and B. Nolan (2000). "Can Gender Differences in Poverty Within Households Be Measured Using Non-Monetary Indicators?", *Feminist Economics*, Vol. 6, No. 3.

Cantillon, B., I. Marx, D. Prost and R. Van Dam (1994). *Indicateurs Sociaux: 1985-1992*, Antwerp: Centre for Social Policy, University of Antwerp.

Canican, M., S. Danzinger and P. Gottschalk (1993). "Working Wives and Family Income Inequality Among Married Couples", in Danziger, S. and P. Gottschalk (eds.) *Uneven Tides: Rising Inequality in America*, New York: Russell Sage Foundation.

Canican, M. and D. Reed (1998). "Assessing the Effects of Wives' Earnings on Income Inequality", *Review of Economics and Statistics*, LXXX, 73-89.

Central Statistics Office (1980). *Household Budget Survey 1973, Detailed Results for All Households*, Dublin: Stationery Office.

Central Statistics Office (1982). *Household Budget Survey 1980, Detailed Results for All Households*, Dublin: Stationery Office.

Central Statistics Office (1989). *Household Budget Survey 1987, Detailed Results for All Households*, Dublin: Stationery Office.

Central Statistics Office (1995). *Household Budget Survey 1994-95, Detailed Results for All Households*, Dublin: Stationery Office.

Coulter, F., F. Cowell and S.P. Jenkins (1992). "Equivalence Scale Relativities and the Extent of Inequality and Poverty", *Economic Journal*, 102, 1067-1082.

Cowell, F. (1995). *Measuring Inequality*, LSE Handbooks on Economics, Hemel Hempstead: Prentice Hall/Harvester Wheatsheaf.

Doris, A. (1998). *An Analysis of the Labour Supply of British Women to their Husband's Unemployment*, Unpublished Ph.D. Thesis, Florence: European University Institute.

Eurostat (1999) *European Community Household Panel (ECHP): Selected Indicators from the 1995 Wave*, Luxembourg: Office for Official Publications of the European Communities.

Forster, M. (2000). *Trends and Driving Factors in Income Distribution and Poverty in the OECD Area*, Labour Market and Social Policy Occasional Papers No. 42, Paris: OECD.

Goodman, A., P. Johnson and S. Webb (1997). *Inequality in the UK*, Oxford: Oxford University Press.

Gosling, A., S. Machin and C. Meghir (1994). "What Has Happened to Men's Wages since the mid-1980s?", *Fiscal Studies*, 15, 63-87.

Hagenaars, A., K. de Vos and M.A. Zaidi (1994). *Poverty Statistics in the Late 1980s: Research Based on Micro-data*, Luxembourg: Office for Official Publications of the European Communities.

Jenkins, S.P. (1991). "The Measurement of Income Inequality", in Osberg, L. (ed.), *Economic Inequality and Poverty: International Perspectives*, New York: Sharpe.

Jenkins, S.P. (1995). "Easy Estimation Methods for Discrete-Time Duration Models", *Oxford Bulletin of Economics and Statistics*, 57 (1), 129-137.

Juhn, C., K. Murphy and B. Pierce (1993). "Wage Inequality and the Rise in Returns to Skill", *Journal of Political Economy*, 101 (3), 410-42.

Juhn, C. and K. Murphy (1997). "Wage Inequality and Family Labour Supply", *Journal of Labor Economics*, 15, 72-97.

Katz, L. and K. Murphy (1992). "Changes in Relative Wages, 1963-1987: Supply and Demand Factors", *Quarterly Journal of Economics*, 107(1), 35-78.

Layard, R. and A. Zabalza (1979). "Family Income Distribution: Explanation and Policy Evaluation", *Journal of Political Economy*, 87, 5, Part 2, 133-61.

Layte, R., B. Maitre, B. Nolan, D. Watson, J. Williams and B. Casey (2000). *Monitoring Poverty Trends: Results from the 1998 Living in Ireland Survey*, Working Paper, Dublin: The Economic and Social Research Institute.

Levy, F. and R. Murnane (1992). "US Earnings Levels and Earnings Inequality: A Review of Recent Tremds and Proposed Explanations", *Journal of Economic Literature*, 30(3), 1333-81.

Lundberg, S., R.A. Pollak, and T.J. Wales (1997). "Do Husbands and Wives Pool Their Resources?", *Journal of Human Resources*, 32 (3), 463-80.

Machin, S. and J. Waldfogel (1994). *The Decline of the Male Breadwinner: Changing Shares of Husbands' and Wives' Earnings in Family Incomes*, STICERD Working Paper No. WSP/103. London: London School of Economics.

Murphy, D. (1984). "The Impact of State Taxes and Benefits on Irish Household Incomes", *Journal of the Statistical and Social Inquiry Society of Ireland*, Vol. XXV: 55-120.

Murphy, D. (1985). "Calculation of Gini and Theil Inequality Coefficients for Irish Household Incomes in 1973 and 1980", *Economic and Social Review*, Vol. 16: 225-249.

National Economic and Social Council (1990). *A Strategy for the Nineties: Economic Stability and Structural Change*, Report No. 89, Dublin: National Economic and Social Council.

Nolan, B. (1978). "The Personal Distribution of Income in the Republic of Ireland", *Journal of the Statistical and Social Inquiry Society of Ireland*, vol. XXIII: 91-139.

Nolan, B. (1981). "The Redistribution of Household Income in Ireland by Taxes and Benefits", *Economic and Social Review,* 13 (1), 59-88.

Nolan, B. (1986). "The Distribution of Social Security Transfers in the UK", *Journal of Social Policy,* 15 (2), 185-204.

Nolan, B. (1998). *Low Pay in Ireland*, Volume II of the Report of the National Minimum Wage Commission, Dublin: Stationery Office, 1998.

Nolan, B. and T. Callan (1989). "Measuring Trends in Poverty Over Time: Some Robust Results for Ireland 1980-1987", *Economic and Social Review*, 20, 309-328.

Nolan, B. and T. Callan (eds.) (1994). *Poverty and Policy in Ireland*, Dublin: Gill and Macmillan.

Nolan, B., R.M. Hauser and J.P. Zoyem (2000). "The Changing Effects of Social Protection on Poverty", in Gallie, D. and S. Paugam (eds.), *European Welfare Regimes and the Experience of Unemployment*, Oxford: Oxford University Press.

Nolan, B. and D. Watson (1998). *Women and Poverty in Ireland*, Dublin: Oak Tree Press.

Nolan, B., C. Whelan and J. Williams (1998). *Where Are Poor Households? The Spatial Distribution of Poverty and Deprivation in Ireland*, Dublin: Oak Tree Press.

Nolan, B., G. Boyle, T. Callan, A. Dorris, I. Kearney, J. FitzGerald, S. Machin, D. O'Neill, J. Walsh, J. Williams, B. McCormick and D. Smyth (1999). *The Impact of the Minimum Wage in Ireland*, published in Final Report of the Inter-Departmental Group on the Implementation of a National Minimum Wage, Dublin: Stationery Office.

O'Donnell, R. and C. O'Reardon (1996). "The Irish Experiment", *New Economy*, 3 (1), 33-38.

O'Neill, D. and O. Sweetnam (1998) *Poverty and Inequality in Ireland, 1987–1994: A Comparison using Measures of Income and Consumption*, Department of Economics Working Paper, Maynooth: NUI Maynooth

Organisation for Economic Co-Operation and Development, (1990). *Employment Outlook*, Paris: OECD.

Organisation for Economic Co-Operation and Development (1990). *Revenue Statistics*, Paris: OECD.

Organisation for Economic Co-Operation and Development (1993). *Employment Outlook,* Paris: OECD.

Organisation for Economic Co-Operation and Development (1996a). *Education at a Glance: OECD Indicators*, Paris: OECD.

Organisation for Economic Co-Operation and Development (1996b). *Employment Outlook*, Paris: OECD.

Roche, J. (1984). *Poverty and Income Maintenance Policies in Ireland*, Dublin: Institute for Public Administration.

Rottman, D. and M. Reidy (1988). *Redistribution Through State Social Expenditure in the Republic of Ireland 1973-1980*, Report No. 85, Dublin: National Economic and Social Council.

Schmitt, J. (1995). "The Changing Structure of Male Earnings in Britain, 1974-88", in Freeman, R. and L. Katz (eds.), *Differences and Changes in Wage Structures*, Chicago: University of Chicago Press.

Shorrocks, A.F. (1980). "The Class of Additively Decomposable Inequality Measures", *Econometrica*, 48, 613-625.

Shorrocks, A.F. (1982a). "Inequality Decomposition by Factor Components", *Econometrica,* 50, 193-211.

Shorrocks, A.F. (1982b). "The Impact of Income Components on the Distribution of Family Income", *Quarterly Journal of Economics*, 98, 311-326.

Shorrocks, A.F. (1983). "Ranking Income Distributions", *Economica*, 50, 3-17.

Shorrocks, A.F. (1984). "Inequality Decomposition by Population Sub-Groups", *Econometrica,* 52, 1369-1385.

Wood, A. (1994). *North-South Trade, Employment and Inequality: Changing Fortunes in a Skill-driven World*, Oxford: Clarendon Press.